THE DEPLORABLES' GUIDE TO FAKE NEWS

By Nick Harlow

D1566826

This is a work of sarcasm and satire. Any resemblance of biased reporters to real journalists is pure fiction.

FAKE PRAISE FOR "THE DEPLORABLES' GUIDE TO FAKE NEWS"

"The author's basic playbook on fake news leaves biased reporters more exposed than a certain former Congressman on Twitter."
    -Campaign strategist Jerry Mander

"When I was a kid mom yelled at me for making up stories. Now I make big bucks doing just that. This book shows how easy it is!"
    -Mainstream media print reporter Paige Turner

"The best book ever—" (quote taken out of context)
    -Congressman Phil E. Buster

"Drives a stake through the heart of political correctness! Will make a millennial's head explode!"
    -Psychologist Noah Fence

NOVELS BY NICK HARLOW

The Girl in the White House
Hit List
The Brokered Convention
Endgame
The Ascendant
The End
The Race
The Sixteenth Minute
Public Affairs
The Infinity Code

ACKNOWLEDGMENTS

While this book did not take years of research (or even days), it did take decades of observation. I've spent a career as a television reporter and network field producer while also taking a few years off to run political campaigns, so I've been on both sides of the fence and seen a lot. I know both playbooks.

But nothing compares to the incredible volume of garbage being put out by news organizations these days. This book would not be possible without the cooperation of the mainstream media who have provided the country with a mountain of steaming crap. As someone who has worked thirty years in the news business, and who has tried my best to always remain objective and unbiased, I personally find the lack of professionalism among the media very hard to understand... and embarrassing to those of us working in the industry who try to remain ethical. Maybe this book will get some of those biased reporters to wake up and remember the basic tenets of the job. But I doubt it. They don't like being criticized, and are more thin-skinned than any politician.

Before bubble-wrapped kids descended on Ivy League colleges, they were the original precious snowflakes.

But no book is written without help. Special thanks to those reporters, editors and all those in the news business who conveniently forgot their first class of Journalism 101 and believe that being biased and slanting a story qualifies as objectivity. Without their selective memory, inability to ask a fair question, and their tireless, herculean efforts to push their agenda on the general public (known in newsrooms as "the great unwashed masses" or "flyovers"), this book would not be possible.

I owe a debt of gratitude to Natasha the Russian operative (probably not her real name), who I met when I took a wrong turn in an office building and wound up in a meeting room. She now runs a support group known as BFD (Blamed For Defeat) made up of former Russian spies and hackers who are now forced to live in the shadows. These people are currently in group therapy trying to deal with being the only ones blamed for Hillary's loss by the media and Democrats in a blameless society that refuses to take responsibility for anything.

Natasha turned me on to her group's nemesis, an organization known as FUBAR (Furious Underlings Blaming All Russians.) Members of this group remain in denial that a candidate with more baggage than a trophy wife on a European vacation lost the 2016 election. They strive to come up with any possible excuse for the loss except the obvious one and have the media promote their narrative. So they get a thank you for keeping fake news alive. (Remember, excuses are little lies you tell yourself.)

Politicians, of course, are also a key, as they have learned how easily the media can be manipulated. And how the media can be used to promote their agenda. So their "efforts" helped make this possible.

And the term "fake news" would not have taken off without our new President. So he gets a big thank you. (And a free copy, should the Commander-in-Chief want one. Operators are standing by.)

Finally, (this is the serious part) I owe a huge debt of gratitude to both my journalism professor and various television news directors who taught me to check my opinions at the door and that it was my job to tell people what I know, not what I think.

Makes it a lot easier to spot fake news.

Now, it's time you learned how to do the same.

WELCOME TO FAKE NEWS 101!

Let's face it, trusting the mainstream media these days is like hiring Anthony Weiner to babysit your daughter.

Yes, if you're a conservative you'd probably feel more comfortable dealing with a used car salesman in a polyester suit than believing the stuff you see on television or read in the newspapers.

And you've no doubt heard the relatively new term "fake news" thrown about with regularity.

Hence, this guide to help you recognize something that's as fake as a Chinese knockoff Rolex sold on a New York street corner.

But while the term "fake news" might be in its infancy, the concept goes way, way back. It used to be a lot more subtle, almost subliminal. A negative adjective here, an unflattering photo there, and that pretty much did the job. The difference now is that it has become so obvious, so totally naked and in your face, that it has pretty much destroyed the reputation of the news business. When you have one of the hosts of a network morning show vacationing with a former Democratic President in an exotic locale, well, it's not like the mainstream media is trying to hide where their loyalties lie. And social media has definitely helped fuel the fires, spreading rumors faster than the speed of light. While there are still a lot of fair, objective reporters out there, the ones who make a really good living putting out faux stories have pretty much buried any trust the general public had in journalism. Very sad, since journalists were originally supposed to be the gatekeepers of the public trust.

Why has fake news become such an epidemic? Several reasons.

Years ago people had one newspaper swat their front door in the morning and they watched one newscast at night.

Now, the internet has provided an unlimited amount of reading material. The news doesn't just come from trained journalists, but from anyone who wants to post a story. And the internet is forever. You can't un-ring that bell. Stories which might sound plausible can zip around the planet at warp speed. Rumor often becomes fact, at least on the internet. Perception is reality.

Throw in twenty-four hour cable news stations, and you've got the general public wondering what's real and what isn't. Major stories covered by one news organization aren't even mentioned on others, or covered with a completely different slant.

So how do you know what to believe?

Well, turn the page and I'll share the fake news playbook. To recap how this took off like a rocket, we're going to start in the wardrobe department...

CHAPTER ONE:

FIFTY SHADES OF GRAY PANTSUITS

"If Hillary Clinton came to an abrupt halt, a reporter would break his nose."

Domination isn't just for the movies and books anymore.

Perhaps the image which told me the media had lost its collective *cojones* when covering Democrats was the one showing the Clinton campaign actually herding reporters and photographers with a rope as the candidate headed down the street. If you haven't seen this video, you need to look it up. Anyway, out of all these people assigned to cover the campaign, out of all these supposedly tough reporters, no one did anything about it. They may as well have uttered a collective "moo" as they followed the trail boss.

Their spines headed for slaughter.

Back in the day, just about any photographer I worked with would have simply taken out a pocket knife and cut the rope. Any reporter, myself included, would have simply ducked under the rope. While you always respect the parameters set by the Secret Service and law enforcement, reporters know they'd never pull this kind of stunt. To let yourself be treated this way is inexcusable and shows a lack of backbone. All it would have taken was for one member of the media to stop, say, "Get rid of the rope or we're not shooting a damn thing," and the giant lasso would have disappeared. But reporters who are famous for standing up for their First Amendment rights and have gone to jail to protect a source did nothing and submitted. Those in the campaign who came up with the idea must have been laughing at how complicit the media was.

While this was probably amusing to most people who saw it and got an eye roll from the journalists who wouldn't stand for such a thing, the coverage was predictable. And while some in the mainstream media did complain that this was "bad optics" for the Clinton campaign, if this had been done by a Republican candidate, they would have dug up some old black and white clips from classic westerns with cowboys herding cattle and played that old Gene Autry song "Back in the Saddle Again." I can only imagine the headlines:

Welcome to the Trump campaign: Head 'em up, move 'em out.
GOP unveils new media rope-a-dope tactics.
Reporters all tied up covering Republican nominee.
Blazing saddles: media fumes at being treated like cattle.
Republicans leave reporters at the end of their rope.

Yes, many members of the mainstream media let themselves be dominated in the last campaign. Not in an erotic novel fashion, of course, but those controlling them may as well have rolled over and lit up a cigarette. The media still pretty much did as they were told. While they weren't literally handcuffed, their hands were basically tied when it came to covering liberal candidates.

"Nothing to see here" became a popular line to discourage reporters who might be looking into something which could have been damaging to a liberal candidate. It's like a grocery store saying, "Sorry, we're out of bread, come back tomorrow." In this case, the campaign was always out of bread.

That might have been fine, except the sisterhood and brotherhood of the traveling pantsuits were thrown a curve ball in the form of a socialist who wasn't even an official member of the Democratic Party. The coronation that had been written into the script was being upended by a guy who spoke with a wicked *Noo Yawk* accent and had hair combed by an eggbeater who for some odd reason was popular with kids fifty years younger.

Actually, the reason wasn't odd at all. He was promising free stuff.

Kids love free stuff.

Plus, he actually seemed like he was telling the truth about his beliefs.

Now came the hard part. The mainstream media had to look like they were being fair.

Problem was, hard to downplay a guy attracting thousands more at campaign rallies than the heir apparent. This was the definition of a true grass roots movement.

And while everyone assumed the wild-haired guy would soon be tapping trees for maple syrup back in Vermont and yelling at kids to get off his lawn, the fairness thing got another curve ball in the form of something called *superdelegates*.

Ah, the superdelegate, that high level member of the party who can vote for anyone at the convention, primary results be damned. You won the primary with ninety percent of the vote to my ten percent? Sorry, I got all the superdelegates.

You want an example of something that young people say is *so not fair*? Look no further.

This was the ultimate shade of gray pantsuit.

Turns out one candidate had a ton of these in her pocket, sorta like an old fashioned head start you might have gotten in a grade school race. It would be like spotting the New England Patriots ten points before the game started along with the other team's playbook. In this case, the playbook came in the form of questions given to one candidate before a debate.

Campaign strategist: The guy with the accent won another primary. He's promising free college and people are believing him.

This could play havoc with our coronation plans. I already commissioned a crown. Should I put the order on hold?

Party bigwig: Nothing to worry about.

Campaign strategist: I dunno, free college is very appealing to kids with student loans living in mom's basement. How about we promise free cars?

Party bigwig: Don't need to. We've got control of all the superdelegates. And we, uh, kinda know what the questions are for the debate.

Campaign strategist: The people supporting the guy with the accent will be angry. They'll say the fix is in. They'll wonder why we have primaries or debates at all.

Party bigwig: Hey, he knew the rules of the game before he threw his hat in the ring. Besides, we can always fall back on the fact that he's not actually a member of the party. Now go ahead and get the crown.

The mainstream media did touch on the superdelegate thing, explaining how it works, but that didn't delete the impression that the whole primary process was rigged. And it didn't appease the followers of the guy with the free stuff. The media shoved the issue quietly to the back burner. Which they assumed was turned off.

But wait, we found more pantsuits in the closet!

Except these are the ones for the charity pile.

Turned out Wikileaks had a whole wardrobe in the attic, tossing out incriminating ugly pantsuits a little at a time like someone doing spring cleaning and gathering stuff for Goodwill.

And while the mainstream media did cover these hacked emails, the main focus was that... wait for it... *they were stolen.* Forget that the Democratic Party would not deny the content, *the emails were stolen.* Which is sorta like saying, "Yeah, I shot the guy and killed him, but the gun wasn't mine." (Note to reader: if you want to prevent your computer from being hacked, "password" is not a strong password.)

By the end of the campaign, all the shades of pantsuits were on full display for the voters. And while the mainstream media kept its own pantsuits cleaned and pressed, it's clear that like a blood drop on white linen, some stains just don't come out.

Which made it hard to broadcast fake news that people would actually believe.

CHAPTER TWO:

BAD WORDS MATTER

Wiretapping: Electronic eavesdropping accomplished by seizing or overhearing communications using a concealed recording or listening device connected to the transmission line.

That's just one of the definitions you can find about the word "wiretapping." And over the years Hollywood has portrayed the process with a reel-to-reel tape recorder hooked up to a phone line with alligator clips while a couple of feds are listening in.

The key word in the definition above is "eavesdropping." Everyone knows what that means. Doesn't really matter how it's done these days, and personally, I have no idea what technology or methods people are using to spy on someone or on foreign countries. I'm pretty sure the media doesn't know either as governments aren't likely to share that information. What constitutes electronic eavesdropping these days? How can you connect to a transmission line or hack the internet? And are they still doing old school stuff like bugging someone's office with hidden microphones?

We all know exactly what the President meant when he used the word *wiretap*. He obviously meant surveillance. While all wiretapping is spying, not all spying is wiretapping. And since he's of the older generation as I am, the term "wiretap" is the term we grew up with when it comes to surveillance. Either that term or "bugging" which was popular during the whole

Watergate thing. How it was done does not matter in the least. *If it was done matters a lot.* It's not the process, but the act.

But the mainstream media seized on that one word, and, in an ironic twist, called it fake news. Even worse, a lie. (Of course, they'd never admit that fake news is basically a lie that is broadcast or printed. But as we are learning in Fake News 101, the rules don't apply to the mainstream media. Just everyone else. Their members are infallible, like the Pope.)

Someone may have hacked the internet at Trump Tower, used some digital technology to intercept a phone call, cloned a cell phone or done something we've never heard of in order to listen to a conversation. Someone might have planted a running tape recorder in a room or installed a hidden microphone. A person could have worn a wire or had a cell phone in a pocket recording a conversation. But all the media cared about was that "wiretapping" by the strict definition of the word (a definition they chose) was not done, that no one actually hooked up physical wires and a tape recorder to an actual old fashioned telephone land line. You heard the statement countless times. "But no *wiretapping* was actually done."

The mainstream media loves to play the semantics game and will seize on one word in an attempt the change the meaning or the narrative. Things that are obvious violent acts of radical terrorism are often blamed on a "lone wolf." The Fort Hood massacre was an incident of "workplace violence." It's as if the media believes that changing the words will make these terrible events less horrific.

And they'll jump on a conservative whose words can be brought into question, even if it's something simple.

Republican on Sunday morning show: I'm concerned that foreign tuna boats are killing dolphins. I'm introducing legislation to protect those fish.

Host: A dolphin is a mammal.

Republican: Whatever. You know what I mean.

Host: But you called a dolphin a fish. That's a lie.

Republican: It swims, it's in the ocean, it's a fish, okay? The fish and wildlife people know what I mean.

Host: But do the fish and wildlife people look after mammals? It is called FISH and wildlife. Not mammals and wildlife. So you really have no idea what you're talking about—

Republican: For God's sake, I just want people to stop killing Flipper!

Another term the mainstream media jumped on was "alternative facts". That doesn't mean things which are lies, just facts that are different. And yes, there can be differing facts on any issue.

Take the whole global warming climate change thing. Many scientists have presented meteorological facts supporting the theory. Many other scientists have presented meteorological facts debunking it. You might even call them "alternative facts" if you are so inclined. Doesn't mean that any of the scientists are lying, or that their research isn't backed up by facts, it just means that there are very often many ways to look at things, depending on how you interpret the information.

Political polls are a fine example of providing alternative facts. The mainstream media can use actual polling numbers showing a conservative is unpopular. But others can take the same poll and use the fact that it sampled twenty percent more Democrats than Republicans. Anyone can cherry pick numbers out of a poll. Those alternative facts are still true, but a different way of looking at things and interpreting information.

Now, let's look at how a single word can change a story. The mainstream media has raised the use of adjectives to an art form. Here's an example of how one word can affect your overall impression of a news item:

Accurate story: Mayor Jones said that he is working hard in an effort to reach an agreement with the city's unions.

Biased story: Embattled Mayor Jones said that he is working hard in an effort to reach an agreement with the city's unions.

See how the word "embattled" led you to believe the Mayor is under fire, fighting off people at every turn? Maybe he is, maybe he isn't, but it's not the reporter's job to add an opinion to the story with that one word. To the average viewer or reader who doesn't pay close attention to the news, the impression is that the Mayor is having problems and is under siege. Let's look at another example regarding newspaper headlines:

Accurate headline: White House staff members offer differing ideas on health care

Biased headline: Health care arguments leave White House in turmoil

A few changed words and the tone of the headline is completely different. If you pick up a newspaper and see the first headline, you'll assume that the higher ups in the White House are discussing different ways to approach health care reform, and that they're working on it. If you read the second one, you envision knock down drag out arguments with people yelling and screaming at one another while lamps are flying across the room. (Supposedly a trend in a previous administration.) And of course the whole purpose of the biased headline is to make the guy at the top look like he's running a dysfunctional administration.

Finally, there are those graphics you see at the bottom of your TV screen which sum up the story being discussed. The same concept applies. With so many people on their computers while watching television (the original term was "tele-webbers") and not paying complete attention, a quick look at the bottom of the screen can have the desired effect. "White House Turmoil" can create a negative impression even if you don't hear one word of what's being said.

Bottom line, words matter when it comes to fake news, and it's very simple to change the entire perception of a story with a few well-placed adjectives or verbs.

CHAPTER THREE:

THE MAINSTREAM MEDIA'S STAGES OF GRIEF

It's commonly accepted in the medical community that there are five stages of grief: anger, denial, bargaining, depression and acceptance. It basically goes like this after the doctor says you are about to kick the bucket:

Anger: You're furious that you're going to die.

Denial: This can't be happening to me. The doctor made a mistake. The tests were wrong. I'll get a second opinion.

Bargaining: You go to confession for the first time in 40 years, keep the priest busy for an hour with a laundry list of sins, then propose a deal with God that you'll join the Little Sisters of the Poor if He will cure you.

Depression: You realize you really are going to take a dirt nap, go into a deep funk and start walking in the woods, looking for people who will take a selfie with you, which will hopefully make you look better than you feel.

Acceptance: You accept the fact you will soon reach room temperature, eat as much chocolate as possible and drink all the good booze in the house, while going on a spending spree to leave your children with a massive amount of debt.

Of course if you've never gone through something like this or know someone who has, you probably haven't seen those things up close. Fortunately, we got to see the stages play out on a national scale after the 2016 election, and we didn't even need a medical diagnosis. The only thing necessary was the media spotlighting a bunch of people who had no concept of what it means to actually lose an election. Or to lose, period. Remember, in 2016, everyone was supposed to get a trophy.

So the stage of "acceptance" was outta here, replaced by "more anger" and "refusal to accept."

Anger: She lost? Who the hell voted against her? Who didn't come out to vote at all? Where were all the Bernie supporters? I hate these people.

Denial: She couldn't have lost. Surely there was something wrong with the election. Someone needs to look into this because it is not possible that she lost. The voting machines were obviously hacked. Or a lot of people added wrong. Damn Common Core.

Bargaining: Maybe Congress can overturn the election and appoint Hillary the winner since she won the popular vote. Majority rules, right? They can overrule that Electoral College thing, can't they? Is that stuff really in the Constitution, and who made up that crazy rule? Or, we can have a do-over election. I'll call my member of Congress and see if that will work. Yeah, she actually won!

Depression: It's the end of the world. I have nothing to live for. I've started eating cat food as a form of protest and will not shave until the new President is impeached. I don't even have the energy to walk to my safe space. It probably isn't safe anymore anyway. I'll bet it has been invaded by people with opinions.

More anger: Hey, let's go have a demonstration and do some looting to show the world we're ticked off! That'll show 'em! (Besides, I need a new flat screen TV.)

Refusal to accept: I will not accept this new President and will continue to resist! Still with her! I'm going to wear pantsuits until this thing is overturned! Even though I'm a guy!

Meanwhile, the mainstream media seized on all the stages at once like some ultimate psychological casino buffet and saw the opportunity for a fake news lollapalooza. It had all the ingredients and all the stages were covered. The video of angry people was easy to get, as protests "sprang up spontaneously" all around the country. (Sorta like that Benghazi attack was spontaneous.) The bargaining stage was also low-hanging fruit and highly entertaining, with people screaming for impeachment even before the new President took office. The line of people in denial was longer than the river in Egypt.

And then the denial river got a huge lifeline in the person of Jill Stein and her recounts.

All of a sudden there was a ray of hope. Surely votes were miscounted and Hillary won four more states. This will prove the Republicans cheated and the election will be overturned! Go, Jill, go!

In a heartbeat, a candidate who had been a blip on the radar was lead story for the mainstream media. For several days. Jill Stein was everywhere and it looked like she was on a mission. What few media outlets bothered to cover was who might actually be behind that mission if it wasn't her. Curious that she only started a recount in states which the Republican candidate won. Odd that another Democratic campaign showed up to make sure things were on the level but "didn't want to get involved." And sorta funny that the losing candidate never came out and said, "don't bother" and didn't take the high road like Richard Nixon did in 1960 when it looked like something fishy was going on to elect JFK.

Obviously someone hacked the voting machines! Even those not connected to the internet. Surely the Russians or the Republicans or both went through the entire state of Pennsylvania, machine by machine, and rigged every last one of them to count more Republican votes.

All this for a candidate who had gotten about one percent of the vote.

(By the way, this soon morphed into the rare combination of more anger and bargaining, sort of a seventh stage of grief.)

Alas, the results of all the recounts took the air out of the balloon and sent them back into the depression stage, especially when the recount in Michigan showed a whole bunch of illegal votes in Detroit in a Democratic district. But that got very little coverage since it didn't fit the narrative that the Republicans were the ones who benefited. Seriously, who cares that there were more votes than registered voters? That's not news, right? It didn't matter because once the recount news cycle was over, it was time to go back to that endless fifth stage. Time for more anger? What's a mainstream media anchor to do?

Wait, wait... they found something! This just in... stand by for...

Faithless electors!

And bargaining is... back in the game!

As it turns out, those people chosen for the Electoral College can actually vote for someone else instead of the person they were committed to. Basically they could overrule the countless people who voted in their states. Who knew? So they could all grow a conscience and vote for Hillary. There's still hope!

Annddd... cue another news cycle.

Suddenly mainstream media reporters ran to the history books to find instances of people who had been faithless electors. It could happen! They profiled a few current electors who were considering it. The media announced that some electors were being called and asked to change their votes, which, of course, encouraged more people to call them and even threaten them. (Back to anger again.) The mainstream media kept that wild scenario going for weeks, making liberals circle the calendar for the day in January when the Electoral College members would officially cast their votes. Some networks even had live shots from different states... many speculated that Hillary could still win if only these electors had common sense and voted for her. A few electors announced they were changing their votes. Let's go to church and light a candle asking God to help them make the right decision.

Alas, that one didn't work either. So we went back to the only things the media had left.

More anger and refusal to accept.

And in order to perpetuate the cycle until they can come up with some other obscure constitutional loophole, the media will trumpet the fact that protests are still going on, regardless of how insignificant that protest is. There might only be thirty people at a protest, but if they are screaming loud enough, have a clever chant and excel at shaking their fists at the camera, creative shooting and editing can make it look as though the entire country is heading for Washington DC with torches and pitchforks.

Think of it as stoking a fire. You never let the fire go out, or you'd have to build a new one all over again. Keep it burning even a little, until you can toss another log into the fireplace. By the same token, the fake news that the entire country is enveloped in a massive protest is kept going with continuing coverage.

And trust me, this stage of grief has no end.

CHAPTER FOUR:

SILVER SPOON ACADEMY: THE MAINSTREAM MEDIA'S FARM TEAM

"Some people are born on third base and go through life thinking they hit a triple."
-football coach Barry Switzer

When the daughter of a former President was hired by a major network as a "special correspondent" even though she had no journalism experience, eyebrows were raised. When she was paid a salary of six hundred thousand dollars tempers flared among those she had leapfrogged, which was basically everyone in the news division laboring for a lot less money. (The network probably felt sorry for her, since her parents were, after all, *dead broke* after leaving the White House.) And when she was assigned to interview an animated character for a news program, well, as we say in the business, you can't make this stuff up. High level sources assure me that this hire did wonders for morale among the rank and file. Needless to say her "career" didn't last long.

Looking back, it was basically a rare faux trifecta. Some might say that animated interview was not only fake news, but done by a fake reporter with a fake job.

Okay, time for a pop quiz:

What's the best journalism school in America when it comes to turning out network reporters? Go ahead, take a guess. Columbia? Nope. Northwestern? Uh-uh. Missouri? Sorry.

It's Silver Spoon Academy (known by normal people in the news business as Nepotism University), which enables the privileged set to leap experienced journalists in a single bound. And make a helluva lot more money in the process.

Here's part two of our quiz: What do Chris Wallace, Anderson Cooper, Chris Cuomo, John Dickerson and Mika Brezhinski have in common?

All are children of famous people. Chris Wallace is the son of the legendary Mike Wallace. Cooper is Gloria Vanderbilt's son. Cuomo is former New York Governor Mario Cuomo's son. Mika's father worked as National Security Adviser in the Carter administration. John Dickerson's mother was a network reporter.

While some may be hard workers, things like paying dues can be optional. Think the well-connected schlepped around in the middle of nowhere for years on end covering car wrecks and boring city council meetings while making paltry salaries?

Ah, grasshopper, you have much to learn before you may roam the earth.

By the way, Silver Spoon Academy is both a K-through-12 school and a college, so children are indoctrinated at a young age to make sure they'll be able to deal with the commoners. One of the first assignments in grade school is to write a story about a poor family, thereby helping the rich and privileged understand how the other half lives. Here's one that got an A+ and a gold star:

"Once upon a time there was a poor family. The mother and father were poor and the children were poor. The Cordon Bleu chef was poor, the sommelier was poor, the butler was poor and the chauffeur was poor."

Students also go through a very tough curriculum in college to help them cope in the real world. Course studies include *White Guilt, Rules That Apply to Everyone Else, Looking Down on the General Public, and Entitlements Not Provided by the Government*. Students do not receive grades or take tests, as they will more than likely never have to fill out a job application or provide a transcript. Because they'll never really have to look too hard for a job by pounding the pavement like everyone else. Parents take care of opening those doors.

The TV news business is filled with graduates of Silver Spoon Academy, sons and daughters of the well-connected who didn't have to pay as many dues as the average reporter. Or perhaps not pay any at all. Oh, but we're not done. This media "family tree" is so narrow it's really a pine. But the few branches it has often extend back to politics.

You see, there's often a connection between the current government and the media. Did you know a certain White House Press Secretary from a previous administration was married to a woman who, at the same time, worked as a reporter for a major network? Yeah, that's something which was best kept under the rug because it just wouldn't look good. I'm sure they never, ever talked about work at home.

And did you ever notice how many people leave a political job only to turn up on a network as anchors or commentators? How one network anchor actually covered a Presidential candidate for whom he used to work?

No conflict of interest there, huh? Problem was, his White House job occurred more than twenty years before the 2016 election, so a lot of young voters who were in kindergarten at the time probably had no idea there was any kind of connection.

And that's what the media is counting on. That no one will take the time to play reporter and find out where the connections are. They assume the general public is lazy. I know better.

It's called the wall of transparency. Except this one is made of brick. Thankfully, that wall has begun to crumble thanks to two things: the media's obvious, over the top bias, and their examples of bias being out there on the internet forever.

Speaking of playing reporter, how do you find out why a certain media person might have an agenda?

You have to put on your journalism hat and do some old fashioned legwork.

Start with looking up the biography of the media person in question, and those are always easy to find. The background information will tell you a lot. If you see things like an Ivy League diploma instead of a plain old state university, you can be pretty sure that unless this person attended on scholarship, this was probably a child of privilege. And of course, a liberal attitude permeates Ivy League schools, so if the student wanted good grades, well, you have to go along and regurgitate what the professor believes. Are that person's parents regular working people, or those who are in some way connected to government or the media?

Want to dig a little deeper? You've heard of the term "guilt by association?" Check out the person's Facebook and Twitter accounts. The type of friends and followers should be a clear indicator of where that person's political sentiments lie. Associations can tell you a lot.

Finally, the thing that would have gotten me fired in a heartbeat years ago: political contributions. I nearly fell off my chair last year when I heard a story that more than ninety percent of media people who contributed to a political campaign did so on behalf of Democratic candidates. Are you kidding me? Someone please explain to me how you are supposed to objectively cover someone when you're contributing to their campaign or any campaign for that matter. This was strictly forbidden years ago, but now it seems commonplace. Anyway, political contributions are public record and easy to look up.

As for the bias genetics, you don't need one of those ancestry.com searches to find out the origins of fake news. In many cases, it's a family tradition.

CHAPTER FIVE:

THE ORIGINS OF "EVERYBODY GETS A TROPHY"

We are constantly bombarded with stories about young people who feel entitled and/or disenfranchised. (One of the favorite words of the mainstream media. Can't get what you want? You're "disenfranchised.") Many people, especially those of a certain age who actually walked to school in the freezing cold (uphill, both ways), often wonder how we got to this point.

But did you ever wonder where the whole concept of "participation" trophies and certificates began?

Well, it's an interesting story...

Once upon a time there was a parent who knew a guy in the Mafia who lived next door. She noted that while he never seemed to go to work, he always got a paycheck and lived very well. Turned out he had what the Mob referred to as a "no-show" job, in which someone is on the payroll but doesn't have to show up for work or do anything. (Kinda like a federal government position, except the Mob has a different procedure when it comes to layoffs.)

Anyway, the parent had a son who had never been on a winning team. And, according to the child's report card, the kid had a great future as a crash-test dummy. His three years in the fifth grade hadn't changed the outlook.

The kid's bedroom walls were bare, with not a single blue ribbon nor a homework assignment with a gold star. Not even a certificate of honorable mention. Not a mention of any kind.

The parent longed for the day when little Johnny would come home with a trophy, or one of those certificates with an embossed gold seal, something she could proudly display in order to show off to the other moms and dads.

And then she thought of the guy in the Mob who lived next door.

He never showed up.

Little Johnny did.

"Hey, if he gets paid for a no-show job, I can take this a step further. Little Johnny shows up... he should get even more!"

And so the parent marched down to the local school board and demanded that all children be treated equally when it came to awards. No more teacher's pets, no more dunce caps. Children should not endure the stigma of being average or below average. They're all special. No one should ever lose, as this would play havoc with her future crash-test dummy's self-esteem. We need to stop keeping score. Why do we even have grades, anyway? They're just arbitrary letters of the alphabet. This request made it to the state legislature, and then went viral, as parents of dim bulb children around the country banded together. It helped that the parent called the mainstream media, who showed up in droves.

They love a good victim, you see.

Just like that, everyone started to get a trophy. Little Johnny's mom had taken a Mafia concept and gotten it implemented into the education system.

And then it filtered down into sports.

No longer would you choose up sides according to who was the best athlete. Every kid got into every game, regardless of athletic ability. Scores didn't matter.

Soon, little Johnny's bedroom walls were filled with certificates of participation he received for just showing up... on those days he actually found the school. It didn't matter that he couldn't read them. His parents could now show off his "accomplishments" to the neighbors. He beamed with pride as he graduated from high school on his 24th birthday, having never lost, having never failed.

And he lived happily ever equal.

Flash forward to the long faces you saw on TV at what was supposed to be a certain campaign "celebration" at three in the morning on Election Night. A whole bunch of people who didn't know what it was like to lose because they had never experienced it, and simply couldn't accept it. Like little Johnny, they thought that simply by participating you should get what you want.

But apparently, according to the Constitution, candidates for President didn't get anything for coming in second.

And thus, when they started whining for the cameras, the fake news story that "she didn't really lose" took hold.

"She got more of the popular vote! So she won, right? What do you mean she still lost? This is so not fair! Who made this rule? Can't we have a do-over like those people in the UK who want to vote on Brexit again?"

Of course you've heard the analogies. That's like saying the Falcons won the Super Bowl in 2017 because they led at halftime.

But the media had picked up the scent like a bloodhound and wouldn't let go. And since there is no such thing as a do-over in presidential elections, there were all sorts of sidebars begging to be done in order to de-legitimize the election and the new President.

-It's time to abolish the Electoral College because the majority should rule.

-There must be a recount out there somewhere that will give us a different result.

-The election was rigged. There's no other way to explain why she lost.

-The new President doesn't have a mandate.

Ah, the "M" word. Mandate. As if that makes a bit of difference to anyone. The President won according to the rules.

But the mainstream media constantly reminded us that he didn't have the "M" word, which is a fake news story in itself.

Yeah, but the new President won the only trophy.

CHAPTER SIX:

THE SUNDAY BIASED BRUNCH BUNCH

"On our diverse panel this morning... a writer from the Huffington Post, a lawyer with the ACLU, a former organizer of Occupy Wall Street, and a medium who will channel the spirit of Ted Kennedy."

Back in the day, Sunday morning was about reading the best newspaper of the week, donuts from the local bakery, coffee on the back porch. Then perhaps a church service, a big family dinner, maybe a football game or a fishing trip. A drive in the family car to take the kids out for ice cream. Sounds pretty relaxing, huh?

That was then, and this is... well...

Stressful.

Now Republicans can start Sunday morning with *agita* (Italian for indigestion) before taking a single bite of that donut. There are political shows at several convenient locations to make your blood pressure spike the moment you roll out of bed if you happen to be conservative. You may as well put a "kick me" sign on your back if you tune into one of these liberal bash-fests designed to make you feel like you're a horrible person because of your views. Oh sure, they might have one conservative on a panel, but that person will often be outnumbered and shouted down by a group that loves to interrupt and goes to great lengths to prevent that person from making a point.

Speaking of interruptions, if you want to see how bad it gets on any show with a panel, turn on your closed captioning sometime. Since these are live shows, the person transcribing the discussion struggles to keep up, and with so many interruptions what ends up on the bottom of your screen often makes no sense. The hosts ought to watch the replays of their shows in this manner, and then maybe they'd actually be able to control the conversation. And the guests might remember their mothers told them it was rude to interrupt.

Of course that assumes the hosts actually *want* to control the conversation. As the old saying goes, "without conflict there is no theater." And conflict is the lifeblood of these shows. Especially when it's three or four against one. Bullying? It's not just for schoolyards anymore.

They'll try to give the show an appearance of objectivity, usually by booking guests from both parties. But it doesn't matter since the panel will usually be stacked with liberals.

Now, here's something important to watch for. Hosts treat conservative guests in the studio a lot differently than those via live shot. And they treat the Democratic guests differently than the Republicans. It's all about body language.

If the guest is in the studio, sitting at the desk across from the host, note if the host is leaning toward the guest. And also note if the host has one hand raised, index finger extended, poised to strike like a cobra.

Ready to attack.

Chances are if you see these things, the studio guest is a Republican.

If the host is leaning back or sitting up straight, no finger ready to strike, chances are the guest is a Democrat.

The tone of the questions is also a tell. Does the host sound combative or conversational? Big difference.

As for the key word during the Sunday morning shows, "but" seems to be it.

Host asks question.

Conservative guest responds.

Host asks follow-up question, the first word of which is "but" and followed by something designed to let the conservative know he's wrong. Imagine a conversation about the budget:

Host: Senator Rightwing, while the proposed tax cuts would supposedly give middle income families a break, how do you justify eliminating the funding for research on the mating habits of the snail?

Senator: (trying not to laugh) Well, we're going to have to cut some items out of the budget because we simply can't justify the expense. I don't think the average taxpayer gives a damn about the romantic aspects of escargot. They only want to see them in garlic and butter sauce.

Host: But... (insert liberal outrage)

Now, to the panel strategy. You know that old saying about wanting the last word? Lots of times they'll give the first word to the conservative, appearing to be polite. And then let the piling on begin.

Host: The big vote on the new health care bill is coming up this week. Republican strategist Joe Patriot, how do you see it?

Joe Patriot: It will really streamline medical care in this country. People will see their premiums go down and the quality of care get better.

Liberal #1: That's because fewer people will be covered after the sick ones die off due to lack of affordable care.

Liberal #2: It's always been the Republican strategy. Push grandma off a cliff.

Liberal #3: And they want to deny health benefits to undocumented immigrants. So you'll be walking over dead foreigners on your way to the emergency room. (wipes a tear) All they wanted (voice cracks) was to live the American dream.

Host: And then, of course, there are the unintended consequences of those fifty-year-olds living in their mother's basements that won't be able to stay on their parents' health care plan.

Liberal #1: That's because their parents will already be dead after going off the cliff.

Host: (laughing along with the liberals) Of course we could discuss this all day, but we're out of time.

Technically, Sunday morning shows aren't newscasts but discussions about the big stories of the week. However, if the host is already biased and is driving the conversation in a panel stacked with liberals, it's easy for fake news to take hold.

CHAPTER SEVEN:

GENERATION SNOWFLAKE

What's a precious snowflake's favorite wine?
"I want to go to my safe space. Waaaa..."

As far as naming a generation goes, "precious snowflake" has to be one of the best labels ever created. I'm not sure who actually came up with the term, but that person should receive the Nobel Prize for snark. Step aside baby boomers, and generation-X. There's a new group in town, one which believes there is more than one center of the universe. And they see it in their mirrors every day.

If you grew up in a place where it snows, as I did, you remember the grade school teacher telling you that snowflakes are unique six-sided crystals and that no two are alike. You might have even looked at snow under a microscope, or seen photos of snowflakes.

You might also have learned that when snowflakes melt, about ten inches of snow will generally equal one inch of water.

Same holds true of our entitled millennials. When human snowflakes who are shown on newscasts melt down, as they do with amazing regularity if you even look cross-eyed at them, you basically get one tenth of a normal person's amount of common sense. However, ten percent might be a generous estimate as any common sense may have long evaporated like snow in July.

Of course, you can't put all the blame on the snowflakes, because someone had to raise them that way. Their parents told them they were unique and special, that the world revolved around them and not the sun, that they were entitled to explore their own path and express their individuality in any manner. Back in the day, this was known as "finding yourself" which resulted in a whole lot of people from my generation ending up with useless degrees and then backpacking across Europe only to return and find that Fortune 500 companies had no need for people degreed in sociology or poetry. Of course, useless degrees are now back in vogue, as we have a whole bunch of kids graduating from college who are well versed in things like Greek mythology or Gender Studies. (An institution of higher learning's version of a participation trophy.) One can only imagine parents who have shelled out fifty grand per year in tuition wondering why their unique spawn can't find a job and have to move back home.

That squeaky sound you hear is a recent graduate pulling out the sleeper sofa in mom's basement.

Which leads us to another cool term for which I cannot take credit: "basement grads."

So, mom and dad, you know that empty nest you thought you were getting for your two hundred grand? How you were going to box up the massive collection of participation trophies and turn the kid's bedroom into a man cave or an art studio? Is it getting a little chilly in the house? That's because there's a snowflake in the forecast.

For the first time in history, it is snowing *inside* a home.

And wouldn't you love to be a fly on the wall when these kids go job hunting with a useless degree?

Employment agency manager: So, what sort of job are you looking for?

Basement grad: (looking up from cell phone) Can I have your phone number so I can text you the answer?

Employment agency manager: No. There's an old form of communication called talking, maybe you've heard of it?

Basement grad: (rolling eyes) Whatever. Well, my degree is in ancient philosophy, so I'd like a management position where I can impart two thousand year old wisdom on my co-workers while maintaining a safe space for others to express themselves without fear of criticism.

Employment agency manager: I see. Are you familiar with the term, "You want fries with that?"

But here's the one thing snowflakes have going for them. The mainstream media loves them.

Because they believe the same thing the media does.

That the country is, to use one of their favorite excuses, *so not fair*.

Safe spaces, micro-aggressions, trigger warnings, the inability or refusal to accept defeat (those damn participation trophies rear their ugly heads once again) and their amazing ability to shout down anyone who thinks differently. They make good copy and viral video. No such thing as a slow news day when you have a conservative speaker being booed off the stage at a liberal college.

But the absolute best thing they have going for them?

They're victims.

Actually, not real victims. Perceived victims.

Victims of ridiculous student loans, conservatives with opinions on campus, no separate bathrooms for undocumented immigrant bungee jumpers, you name it. If there's a liberal cause that isn't going exactly the way they want, they're angry and upset. They have been wronged and they are not shy about telling the whole world. In very loud voices.

Because things are... wait for it... *so not fair*.

Heroes are fine, but victims can garner sympathy. And the mainstream media will go to great lengths to showcase a snowflake who has been wronged in any way. All they need is one to mount a national campaign. Once they have a poster child for a specific issue, like that illegal alien bungee jumper who bounces between the men's room and the ladies room, they'll use that person to push the agenda. Doesn't matter that the issue affects ten people out of 300 million; *someone* has been wronged. And it's the fault of those closed-minded Republicans.

I often wonder if the mainstream media broadcasts these stories simply to tick off conservatives. If that's their objective, it works.

Well, to a point.

Let's take a break here so you can do a simple internet search for "conservative riot." Nothing? Try "conservative looters." What, no video of patriotic people waving flags as they smash store windows and run off with flat screen televisions? Can't find any video of military veterans throwing rocks at police officers? No clips of senior citizens hurling Molotov cocktails?

The mainstream media would love that kind of viral video. Which is why they often spotlighted an isolated incident at a Trump rally. Of course, we later found out there were liberal groups whose specific goal was to infiltrate the rallies and start a confrontation, but the tenets of fake news dictate that part of the story is ignored. It would make their side look bad.

But the conservative riot or patriotic looting video remains the Holy Grail for the mainstream media. Unfortunately, being angry and breaking the law usually doesn't go together for flag-waving conservatives.

So for now, they'll have to be content with using the snowflakes to create fake news, staged altercations they can broadcast to make conservatives look intolerant. The angrier the snowflakes act on camera, the better. Cue the yelling. It also helps to have a clever chant for the kids to repeat. "Hey, hey, ho, ho, the bungee jumper has gotta go!" Maybe they all wear giant rubber bands around their necks and throw toilet seats to show solidarity.

Oh, and don't forget picket signs, like those pre-printed ones they had ready to go the minute a new Supreme Court Justice was nominated. Cue the protest with a bunch of people who were ready to slam *anyone* the President nominated. Gotta cover all bases so the media can say, "The spontaneous protests against the judge have already begun!" Once again, those "spontaneous" protests are of the Benghazi variety.

Remember, you can always find the lunatic fringe element of any political party. The problem with the extreme wings of both parties is that these people yell the loudest and get the most coverage, thereby stereotyping members of the political factions. The mainstream media likes to show off the conservative wing's tin foil hat members and paint them in a negative light, while their liberal counterparts are always the victims. And not portraying one side's whack jobs for what they truly are is another form of fake news.

Meanwhile, the young people who aren't precious snowflakes, the ones studying hard in college while they wait tables so they can stay out of mom's basement... well, you'll never see them at all. They're not considered "good copy" by the mainstream media. Where's the news value in some kid who isn't mad at the world paying his college tuition by working nights for tips in a restaurant?

Basically, that's like leading your newscast with, "A plane didn't crash today."

Remember, without conflict there is no theater. And the snowflakes always provide the conflict, while the normal kids do not.

CHAPTER EIGHT:

TAKING SOMETHING OUT OF CONTEXT ISN'T JUST ABOUT WORDS ANYMORE

Like many Americans, I watched a lot of the coverage of both the Republican and Democratic conventions. Both featured high points and low ones, great speeches and those more powerful than a bottle of Ambien. It was two weeks of sound bites that could be chopped up and taken many different ways, depending on how they were edited.

But perhaps the most egregious example of something taken out of context wasn't a sound bite. It was a single frame of video from the Republican convention.

Maybe you saw conservative columnist and commentator Laura Ingraham deliver a speech to the GOP. Like most of the speakers, she came out and waved to the crowd. No big deal, right? Well, someone either paused the video or took a photo of her waving, which, at that particular split second in time, captured her with her arm raised, straight out toward the crowd, palm down.

All of a sudden she was accused of giving a Nazi salute. The image went viral.

Are you kidding me? This is a woman who wears her religion on her sleeve in the form of a necklace with a gold cross and is never on TV without it. But now, thanks to one still frame of video, people were calling her a white supremacist giving a salute to a room full of them.

Welcome to the new definition of taking something out of context. In this case, it's actually worse than chopping up a sound bite.

Now I could probably take video of any politician, slow it down, frame by frame, and find something similar. There are thirty frames of video per second, by the way, to illustrate how infinitesimal this can be. So there's plenty from which to choose and you can find the worst image possible. Any editor at any TV station can find the most unflattering frame, copy that one-thirtieth of a second, use it as a graphic, post it on social media, and all of a sudden the subject is ugly, a racist, a sexist, or, in this case, a member of the most heinous group in history.

So we now have a new version of fake news. Video or photos out of context.

Here's another example that happened on inauguration day. The Trumps and Obamas are heading into a building, and Donald Trump is shown walking a few steps ahead of his wife.

Well, one thirtieth of a second and all of a sudden he's a horrible husband. You knew what was coming next: the war on women.

Step back a minute and think about this, especially if you're a guy of that generation.

Whenever my wife and I walk into a building, I'm always a step ahead of her just as we reach it.

Because I'm going to hold the door for her.

It's how moms of my generation raised boys. You hold the door for women. There's nothing sexist about it and has nothing to do with a man's feeling about equality of the sexes. It's simply what a gentleman does. And in order to do that, you have to step ahead of the woman as you reach the door. Trump was probably raised the same way. Sure, someone is always going to hold the door for the President, but perhaps he's in the habit of doing that, as I am. Doesn't really matter why he was a step ahead of his wife. Or why she was a step behind him.

But, as the old saying goes, a picture is worth a thousand words. Today, it's worth a million re-tweets or shares.

And that means it is open season on what might seem to be average video.

Bear in mind that the print media has the capability to cash in on this new trend as well. In that case, the photo on the front page will be staring at you all day and as long as the publication hangs around.

If you want to make someone look angry, just slow down the video frame by frame until you see the most unflattering grimace you can find. Doesn't matter that it has nothing to do with the story. Now you've got an image which conveys the notion that the person is mad. Throw in a headline like, "Candidate Scowls at Crowd During Rally" and you've got a full blown fake news story. The person in question may have stubbed a toe and his face tightened in pain. The point, for the biased media organization, is the end result. Do this a few more times and all of a sudden the person has a reputation as being nasty.

And then there's the cropping technique. If you have a group photo with one unsavory character standing next to a politician you like, simply crop out the bad guy. On the other side of the coin, if you want to highlight the bad guy and eliminate the rest of the good crowd, you can create guilt by association.

Finally, there's the software known as Photoshop. You can pretty much create any image you like, post it on the internet and let it go viral.

Taking a quote out of context has always been a big part of fake news. Now you've got to pay attention to the images, which can be even more damaging.

CHAPTER NINE:

GRIEVANCE COLLECTORS

"No good deed shall go unpunished."
-my former News Director

I once did what I considered to be a very inspirational story about a Vietnam Veteran who was paralyzed from the waist down. What made him special was that he had just achieved a black belt in martial arts. The man so inspired us that we really went the extra mile to make the story the best it could be. Our photographer did a beautiful job shooting and editing the story; all the shots at the beginning of the piece were above the waist as the veteran performed his martial arts moves. Then halfway into the story the camera pulled back for the big reveal that he was in a wheelchair. Here's a wounded war hero with a tough physical challenge not letting anything stop him from achieving his dream. Amazing, right? If this story didn't inspire viewers, nothing would.

Or so I thought.

We felt great after that story aired and I heard from a lot of veterans who appreciated it along with those with physical challenges who found it inspiring. The guy so inspired me that I went home that night determined to work even harder on my stories.

And then I got this call the next day:

"I was offended by your story last night."

Of all the television news stories I had ever put together, I couldn't imagine how anyone could possibly find fault with this one. It was one of those rare stories that profiled a truly special person and made the world a better place. Simply by telling his story. Surely the caller had me mixed up with another reporter, or a story I'd done on another day. And then I heard this:

"You said the veteran was confined to a wheelchair. We are not *confined*, we are *liberated* by wheelchairs!"

You gotta be kidding me.

The caller continued to chastise me for that one word.

And that's when my boss hit me with the quote at the top of this chapter.

That was back in the eighties and my first encounter with what I refer to as *grievance collectors*.

Not familiar with the term? Yeah, but you know the type. People who look for ways to be offended. Actually, they don't just look, but go out of their way to find things hidden under rocks that might upset them. They have raised being offended to an art form. It's like they have some sort of mental metal detector scanning the globe to seek out anything that could be taken the wrong way. Words, signs, whatever. Mostly whatever.

How bad has it gotten? We now have a grievance industry. You think I'm kidding? Some publishers (not this one) actually employ "sensitivity readers" to review books before they are published to make sure they don't contain anything offensive.

You're probably thinking, well, that must be done for stuff like school textbooks.

Nope.

Here's the best part... we're talking about *fiction*. Some publishers are actually reviewing novels to make sure some readers out there don't get their panties in a wad.

Yes, people can now be offended by fictional characters.

(Short pause for you to put this book down for a few seconds and roll your eyes.)

Annddd... we're back.

The thing is, the grievance collectors can often drive a news cycle because the mainstream media loves a good victim. All you need is one person offended about some liberal issue, and the media will be all over it. Very often, for days on end.

Of course if it's a slow news day and no one has been offended for the past twenty-four hours (I know, that's a real stretch) the media will do its best to find someone, anyone, who is up in arms about a liberal issue. And if they can't find that, they'll create the issue. This might be a typical morning newsroom meeting when stories are assigned:

News Director: Okay, who's offended today?

Reporter: Unfortunately, the cupboard is bare. Conservatives haven't done anything in the last twenty-four hours to tick someone off.

News Director: Have you checked with the usual radical fringe groups?

Reporter: Yes, Sir. Sorry, nothing out there. Not even a small protest. No lawsuits either.

News Director: Well, we need to find something.

Reporter: Hey, I've got an idea. I've got a friend who works part-time as a circus clown at children's birthday parties. How about we get him to dress up and show up for his day job as a bailiff at the courthouse. They'll try to send him home and he can claim his rights as a clown have been infringed upon. Then I'll get a bunch of people in clown costumes to protest and a legislator to stand up for the clown. Maybe get business people to wear red noses and floppy shoes in a show of support. Should be great video.

News Director: Sounds like a lead story. Of course it would really help if your friend was a transgender Syrian refugee who entered this country illegally, has a long rap sheet and lives on welfare in a sanctuary city. That would check off all the boxes and make conservative heads explode.

Reporter: I'll see what I can do.

As far as the fake news factor goes, the grievance collectors can pull bogus stuff out of the blue and the mainstream media will turn it into a national story. If it will make conservatives look intolerant, it is news as far as the media is concerned.

CHAPTER TEN:

THE MICRO-AGGRESSION ROSETTA STONE TRANSLATOR

Now that you've been briefed on the fake news pushed by grievance collectors, time to give you a basic primer on the code words that push some of the hot buttons now known as "micro-aggressions." You've probably heard about some institutions of higher whining previously known as colleges. Yes, now simple words that shouldn't be remotely offensive to anyone can now send precious snowflakes into a meltdown situation. In some cases, teachers have been asked not to refer to students as boys and girls, Miss or Mister.

Yet another layer of protective bubble wrap for the young generation.

Of course not all young people bruise as easily as a banana. Most are hardworking kids who are focused on a career goal and realize the real world is a tough place. But by spotlighting those who are emotionally fragile, the mainstream media has created the impression that all young people in college are a bunch of entitled wimps who want to live in a protective bubble.

Remember the old grade school line, "Sticks and stones may break my bones but names will never hurt me?" Well, that's pretty much fiction as far as the media is concerned, as they consider words to be more damaging than a punch in the mouth.

Hence, the origin of politically correct terms that will not offend.

This got started in a big way when Democrats refused to call illegal aliens by that term, instead referring to them as undocumented immigrants. Even though they were, in fact, entering this country without going through the proper channels. Which is, you know, illegal.

So that you'll be prepared should you happen to stumble into a safe space on a college campus, here's a decoder for words and terms which are now deemed horribly offensive to some, with the old term followed by the new:

Boys: Estrogen challenged life forms
   Girls: Testosterone challenged life forms
   Looters: Undocumented shoppers
   Rednecks: Sophistication challenged
   Potheads: Purveyors of legal recreational foliage
   Criminals: Misunderstood legal victims
   Actor: Metamorphosing narcissistic being
   Fart: Flatulent ozone depletion anomaly
   Prisoner: Guest of the state
   Victim: Disenfranchised

Of course more terms will be released as people discover more ways to be offended. And we fully expect some universities to offer degree programs in micro-aggressions, which will prepare young people to be successful agoraphobes.

CHAPTER ELEVEN:

CONSERVATIVE SAFE SPACE

Write whatever the hell you want on this blank page. Go ahead, I won't judge you.

(If you're reading the e-book version, activate Siri, Alexa, Ok Google or whatever talking technology you have and yell something offensive at it.)

CHAPTER TWELVE:

ASK ME NO QUESTIONS, I'LL TELL YOU SOME LIES...

"If you ask a politician a question and he evades it, don't ask another. Simply say nothing and wait. He can't stand dead air and loves the sound of his own voice. He'll start talking again."

-a main network anchor giving advice to reporters while visiting our newsroom

Ever wonder how reporters decide which questions to ask?

Ever wonder why it's sometimes obvious they aren't listening to the answers?

Well, there's another great little nugget from a veteran reporter.

"There are those who listen, and those who wait to speak."

As far as that goes, most reporters get the husband-tuning-out-wife-bobblehead award because they are simply so focused on the next question they aren't paying attention to the answer that is being given. Next time you see a one-on-one interview on television and you get what is known as a two-shot so you can see both people, keep an eye on the reporter if he has a legal pad in his lap. If he's staring at the pad while the politician is answering his question, he's not listening. He's more interested in getting ready with the next question. As far as the reporter is concerned, he's already done his part and will look at the tape later.

And this is why you often don't get a good follow-up question to a surprising answer.

Because the reporter hasn't been listening.

Reporter: "*So, what are some of the things you've learned in your first year as a Senator?*" (*Looks at legal pad one nanosecond after finishing the question.*)

Senator: "*Well, you have to be an expert in dealing with both parties. Working across the aisle is key.*" (*Notices reporter isn't paying attention.*) "*But the most interesting thing I learned was that we really do have space aliens at Area 51. Some are still alive. I had dinner with a lovely creature from Venus last month.*"

Reporter: (*Looks up from legal pad.*) "*With the situation in the Middle East so fragile, what's your plan?*"

Yep, the reporter missed an amazing revelation because he was concentrating on the next question, on waiting to speak, that he didn't listen to the answer. Meanwhile, you're yelling at the TV screen, wanting more information about those Venusians at the Capitol and if the government has spaceships stashed in Nevada.

You'll also see this on the Sunday morning news shows, where the host is so eager to get his question out he is chomping at the bit to ask. Or to simply reiterate his point of view. Pay close attention to the body language... the host is leaning forward toward the guest, mouth half open with words dying to escape, and obviously not caring one bit what the other person is saying.

He's waiting to speak.

As for that legal pad full of notes, if you're a biased reporter looking to take someone down, there are probably a few gotcha questions in there. And while those can be painfully obvious to a viewer, there are a few subtle catch phrases reporters use in an effort to conceal their bias. Remember, it's not just the question, but often what prefaces it. It's all in the presentation, like a meal at an expensive restaurant.

These methods of asking a question will tell you how far their bias goes and expose their opinions.

When you hear a reporter start a question this way:
"With all due respect..."
That's code for "you're full of it."
And there's this popular starting point:
"Do you really believe..."
Which means simply, that the reporter doesn't.
Then there's the nebulous use of the word "people" which requires no source:
"People on Capitol Hill are saying..."
Really? Which people? How about some names? Got a sound bite you can play or an actual quote in a newspaper? The politician really needs to throw this back in the face of the interviewer and demand attribution, and I've noticed lately that some are doing so, especially when the reporter is using an unnamed source in the form of the ever popular "people" in the question.

Here's another one you'll hear quite often:
"There are those who think you're wrong..."
In other words, the reporter thinks you're wrong. Again, who are *those* people?
And finally, one of my all-time favorites:
"Conventional wisdom would say..."
Of course the reporter's superior wisdom says the politician is wrong.

Are you getting the picture here?
Very often it's not just the question, but how it is framed, how the reporter sets it up. The inflection in the voice. The tone. Is the question a simple query, or is it confrontational?

There's also the body language and visual aspects, the latter of which can be set up by whoever is recording an interview. The proper setting can make anyone look bad. Remember one of the first interviews with Sarah Palin, with the reporter appearing to be sitting up just a bit higher and looking down at her over the top of his glasses like some condescending professor? If you looked at that with the sound off and didn't know who the people were, you'd think... teacher and student. But this was a woman running for Vice President.

It not just the content, but the optics and the tone. Back in 1960 people who watched the Kennedy-Nixon debates thought JFK won. Those who listened on radio thought Nixon did a better job. Which proves that the content of what is said is often not the most important part of a story these days.

CHAPTER THIRTEEN:

OPINION JOURNALISM

"Annoy the media: Re-elect Bush"

-1992 bumper sticker from George H.W. Bush's campaign (supposedly his favorite)

The term "opinion journalism" is an oxymoron. There's no such thing.

If you have an opinion in your story, you're not a journalist. People can argue this all they want, but there really is no gray area. You're either objective or not. And if not, you can't call yourself a journalist.

That doesn't stop anyone.

Of course, these "opinion journalists" have figured out a way to get around the basic tenets of the job with a little loophole known as "commentary." Which would be fine, if commentary was all they did, like radio talk show hosts. That's why you'll often hear a disclaimer at the beginning of most talk shows. "The opinions heard on this program are those of the host and do not necessarily reflect those of the staff or management of this station." So the listeners know right up front that what they're hearing is one person's opinion, and not pure journalism. Years ago, many local stations aired a weekly "editorial" at the end of the Friday newscast, usually delivered by the station manager. But viewers got a disclaimer, and they didn't get the editorial from someone in the news department.

The problem becomes most apparent when you have a regular news reporter who occasionally slides into commentary mode, as they often do on those Sunday morning bash-fests or on the twenty-four hour cable outlets. All of a sudden you have a reporter being asked for his opinion, and said reporter is only too happy to give it. And just like that, the reporter is now a commentator and has slid through the loophole to become an "opinion journalist."

The problem is they often conveniently forget they're in commentary mode when they go back to their day jobs being news reporters. So the opinions filter into their stories, the stories get slanted, and the bias becomes obvious.

And here's another problem that's a result of twenty-four hour cable news outlets; you've got to fill all that time with someone on the anchor desk. There are only so many people in a network who can do that, and when those people are on vacation, out sick or on special assignment, you need someone to fill in. So if you're a manager you reach into the news department. Viewers now find a regular reporter pinch-hitting for a commentator, and for an hour or two that reporter gets to voice opinions. The rules of journalism are once again temporarily suspended thanks to the loophole. The reporter may actually be objective when doing his stories, but the role of host or commentator gives him the opportunity to voice those opinions.

And that's where fake news can flourish.

CHAPTER FOURTEEN:

THE REAL "ONE PERCENT"

We heard a lot about the "99 percent" from groups like Occupy Wall Street (if you want a definition of the "great unwashed masses" look no further) and how those evil people who comprised the "one percent" had all the money and were running the country.

But there's a different "one percent" that resides in newsrooms. No, I'm not talking about the highest paid network anchors or the rich people who actually own a network.

We're talking about the search for the tiniest error by conservatives. They might do 99 out of a hundred things right on any given day, or deliver the greatest speech in decades, but the media will seize on the one thing they may have gotten wrong. Their review of the Gettysburg Address would be, "Inspiring speech, but awfully short. Lincoln could have fleshed it out a bit."

Now if you got a 99 on a math test in school and brought it home to your parents, they'd be thrilled. But in the eyes of the mainstream media, conservatives have to be letter perfect. (Liberals are graded on a curve. 50 is considered an A+)

Reporter: Congressman, you're getting high marks on your party's proposed health care legislation and it appears the support among the members of the GOP is unanimous.

Congressman: Yes, we're united on this one and it's gotten a 99 percent approval rating from the public in a poll taken yesterday. It's helped that I and other members of the committee are all physicians.

Reporter: But there is a great deal of concern that the bill does not address smallpox.

Congressman: (chuckling) Uh, there hasn't been a case of smallpox in forty years. The disease has been eradicated.

Reporter: But would you say it's IMPOSSIBLE that smallpox could make a comeback?

Congressman: While anything is possible—

Reporter: Aha!

Republicans find themselves walking on eggshells around the mainstream media trying their best to avoid that one percent which will constitute 99 percent of the coverage. One wrong word, one action that could be taken the wrong way, or something that can portray the person as stupid, and all of a sudden it is the lead story for days. Joe Biden says something ridiculous or inappropriate? Eh, it's just Joe being Joe. But if a conservative does the same thing, the knives come out and the perceived error is played on a loop.

Remember Rick Perry in the 2012 debate forgetting one item on his list and saying, "Ooops." It stuck like glue, replayed *ad nauseam*. His campaign was done. It was later revealed he'd just had back surgery, but the media wasn't going to cut him any slack.

And sometimes, if the media can't find anything that fills the one percent quota on a given day, they'll find something which doesn't really exist. Fake news, meet fake error.

One of the strangest "little things" that had the media bashing Trump over the head was a graphic put out by his campaign in which the opponent was called "Crooked Hillary." Next to a photo of her was a star with the words "most corrupt candidate ever!" inside the star. Looked like a typical campaign graphic.

Except...

The star was a six-pointed one.

The media saw the Star of David.

And all of a sudden, Trump was anti-Semitic.

Didn't matter that his daughter is Jewish, the media played the white supremacist card for days.

The mainstream media has raised seeing things that aren't there to an art form, like those "magic eye" posters you have to stare at for a long time to see the hidden image.

But here's something the mainstream media hasn't figured out: the general public isn't as easy to fool anymore. They know a big issue from a small one... or in many cases, a non-issue. Political commentators often refer to non-issues as "nothing burgers" and as far as conservatives are concerned, the media thinks the public should have a nothing burger for lunch every day.

Speaking of food terms, you might be interested to know that there's one which has been used for years in television newsrooms.

Chicken salad.

No, not what you might have for lunch in the break room.

It refers to an assignment that a reporter feels is a lame excuse for a story. But the News Director still expects him to sprinkle fairy dust on this dog and magically transform it into something interesting. At some point during the day, the reporter will state that he's been assigned a "chicken salad" story.

Meaning he has to make chicken salad out of chicken poop.

But these days, fake news wouldn't even quality as a chicken salad story since it usually contains one percent or less of actual information.

CHAPTER FIFTEEN:

MEDIA MATH & SCIENCE (NEWSROOM COMMON CORE)

Well, we've been talking about percentages, so let's continue with more arithmetic... and some science.

Since we all know that being proficient in math and science is very important to the success of our educational system, you might be interested in the basic mathematical & scientific concepts of every mainstream media news organization:

FAKE NEWS RATIO: The amount of coverage of a fake news story about Republicans is directly proportional to its lack of credibility. (In other words, the more fake the story, the more coverage it gets.)

BIAS BY OMISSION COROLLARY: The amount of coverage given to a story making liberals look bad is inversely proportional to the credibility of the story. (In other words, if it's really bad for Democrats, and the proof is rock solid, you'll never see it anywhere on the mainstream media. The story get spiked and dies a grisly death.)

PYTHAGOREAN THEOREM OF SNARK: In any interview featuring a Republican, a Democrat, and a member of the mainstream media, the hypotenuse will be the level of snark received by the Republican. (In other words, the conservative gets hammered.)

EUCLIDEAN ANGLE HYPOTHESIS: The angle of a story taken by a member of the mainstream media when covering a conservative will be 180 degrees from the actual story.

HIVE MENTALITY SYNCHRONICITY: The percentage of questions on one subject asked by a group of reporters during a news conference is directly proportional to potential damage said questions can inflict on conservatives.

THE ESCAPE HATCH TANGENT: Occurs when a liberal seems to be in trouble during a news conference and is bailed out by a reporter with a question taking the liberal off in another direction during which said liberal can blame conservatives for something.

DISCUSSION PANEL DIVERSITY EQUATION: Five liberals plus one conservative on a mainstream media Sunday morning talk show equals a perfectly diverse panel.

THE AXE-TO-GRIND RATIO: The degree to which a specific reporter is called out by a Republican will determine the level of fake news broadcast by that reporter in the future. (In other words, if Trump slams a member of the media, get ready for a ton of fiction from that reporter.)

THE LEAD STORY HIERARCHY THEOREM: The order of stories in any newscast will be in direct correlation to the degree in which they make conservatives look bad. (In other words, the lead story will be the one that puts Republicans in the worst light.)

THE STILL-FRAME SUBLIMINAL EFFECT: Using an unflattering freeze-frame of a conservative will subconsciously create a negative impression with viewers, even if the subject is physically very attractive and generally accepted to be handsome or beautiful. (In other words, it's possible to make Nicole Kidman look bad.)

STILL-FRAME COROLLARY: Using a retouched, Glamour Shots, perfectly lit image of a liberal will subconsciously create a positive impression for viewers, even if the subject is physically perfect for those "before" plastic surgery ads.

CHAPTER SIXTEEN:

KILLER ESCALATORS AND SHOPPING CART HANDLES

"Coming up on I-Missed-It News, a two-part series on the deadly threat of your kitchen dish scrubbie. DEATH BY THE KITCHEN SINK is up next... a story that could save your life."

What do February, May and November have in common?

To the average person, nothing.

To anyone in the television industry, they're known as "sweeps months." Those are the three months during which ratings are taken for both the networks and local stations, and those ratings are used to determine the rates for advertising. Higher ratings mean you can charge more for commercials, and those rates are established as soon as the numbers come in from sweeps months. Of course you want great numbers for what they call "key demographics" which are people between the ages of 18 and 49 or 25 and 54, the theory being that people within a particular age group will spend the most money. (At least, those not living in mom's basement.) By the way, the demographic for those over the age of 64 is often referred to as the "near-deads." Nice, huh?

That's why you'll see your local TV news stations go all out during these three months with all sorts of special reports which will hopefully appeal to the key demographic they're targeting. And very often, one or more of those reports will feature something seemingly innocent that can kill you because any information about you possibly kicking the bucket often translates to high ratings. "Stairway to Death" will detail the perils of riding escalators. "Killers of Aisle Five" will make you quake in your boots at the thought of picking up deadly germs from a shopping cart handle. And that colorful, innocent looking dish scrubbie? You may be washing your plates with a veritable petri dish containing the black plague. The horror! Hide under the bed! Run for your lives!

Yes, death gets big ratings.

Politicians have noticed this and often use it to shape public opinion. Because even the most remote possibility of something killing you will make you stand up and take notice.

And get mad.

Change the health care law? People will die. (Okay, that's a no-brainer for Democrats. The Republicans balanced it with death spiral and death panels.)

But besides the obvious changes that actually affect your health, you can weave death into just about anything.

Take the Delta Smelt off the endangered list? People will die.

Cut the price of a postage stamp? People will die. (Bad glue, like the kind in *Seinfeld*.)

Fail to regulate cow flatulence regarding global warming? People will die.

Build a wall between the United States and Mexico? People will die. (Though probably from falling while trying to climb it.)

Support anything Republicans want? Now we can take the death scare level up exponentially. You will not only die, but will endure a grisly death while living in a hovel without indoor plumbing. You'll be found half-eaten by your cats three weeks later, be unidentifiable by a medical examiner, and be interred in Potters Field with the simple headstone reading "unknown victim of Republican legislation."

Of course the mainstream media hits the daily double on any legislation in which death, no matter how remote, can be incorporated. They get to broadcast stories about things that can kill you while handing the smoking gun to Republicans. Two birds with one stone, as it helps ratings and hurts conservatives.

Of course no fake news story would be complete without an appropriate victim, the search of which becomes a team effort between liberals and the media. Once you can put a sympathetic face to a cause, and broadcast the fact that said face will soon be in a coffin, you're good to go.

Liberal Strategist: We need a poster child to fight this proposed Republican legislation which will stop requiring public schools to offer kale in the cafeteria.

Mainstream Media Reporter: Kids eat kale?

Liberal: Apparently not. A million dollar survey by the Department of Education shows 99 percent of it gets thrown out. The other one percent gets taken home by the gym teachers.

Reporter: Not surprised. I think that stuff is Soylent Green.

Liberal: Anyway, kids could die without kale.

Reporter: That's a real stretch.

Liberal: Get me a cute kid who loves kale and a doctor who will say a kale deficiency can result in death.

Reporter: I'll get a pretty little blonde girl. As you know, the public only cares about beautiful female blonde-haired children. It's the network policy regarding child abductions. We don't cover brunettes, boys, minorities or ugly kids. Viewers respond to pretty things that are broken.

And that last thing is the key. The victim has to evoke sympathy on some level. If the victim was a toothless chain smoker wearing the fall collection of Occupy Wall Street, you're not gonna get much support. Keep the "disenfranchised" attractive and fragile, and you've won the fake news battle before it starts.

CHAPTER SEVENTEEN:

RULES NEED NOT APPLY TO CERTAIN GROUPS

Hypocrite: A person who pretends to have certain beliefs but does not actually possess them.

Political hypocrite: A person who pretends to have certain beliefs when it is politically convenient, often overlooking the polar opposite behavior in the past.

You probably heard about that vacant Supreme Court seat which came open after the death of the legendary Antonin Scalia. Since this happened in the final year of a lame duck President's term, the Senate refused to give a hearing to the person chosen by the President. The Democrats were up in arms about this, and the mainstream media banged the drum on this story all year. The seat was being stolen, this was unprecedented, it was an outrage. And after a Republican took the White House, Democrats contended that the seat should remain open forever.

Of course, the other half of the story that didn't get covered very much was something known as "The Biden Rule."

You know Uncle Joe, our most lovable Vice President of all time. The polar opposite of Dick Cheney, who would never be described as "warm and fuzzy." The guy prone to often hilarious gaffes but who seemed like one of the few decent human beings in Washington.

Yep, the Biden Rule was named after Joe back when he was a Senator from Delaware.

Because he said this in 1992, during the final year of President George H.W. Bush's term:

"It is my view that if a Supreme Court Justice resigns tomorrow, or within the next several weeks, or resigns at the end of the summer, President Bush should consider following the practice of a majority of his predecessors and not... and not... name a nominee until after the November election is completed."

That came back to bite the Democrats big time in 2016 when Scalia passed away. As a result, the Republican controlled Senate would not consider a nominee until after the November election. The process would proceed just as Biden had suggested. And what made it even worse was that Senator Biden was now Vice President Biden. (The irony of the Biden Rule was that his statement was made in a year when an opening never occurred anyway. Which was later filed under "what was he thinking?")

Of course, while this was just fine with Democrats in 1992 who sought to block President Bush just in case there was a vacancy on the Supreme Court, now it was an absolute outrage. The Republicans were trying to steal a seat by keeping the Democrats from filling it. And indeed, when Justice Neil Gorsuch was confirmed in 2017, the liberals screamed it had indeed been stolen.

A prime example of rules applying to the Republicans when it was politically convenient, but not to the Democrats, who suffered from selective memory when it came to the Biden Rule.

So, let me get this straight. If we're in the last year of a Republican President's term then a Supreme Court nomination should not be made, but if the President is a Democrat, by all means let's confirm the nominee.

Got it?

While the mainstream media did mention the Biden Rule on occasion, they booked a parade of Democrats on various shows and let them scream about the supposedly stolen seat. Oh, and something else that was barely mentioned? There had been Supreme Court Justices confirmed with less than sixty votes in the past before the so-called "nuclear option" was invoked by the Senate. Democrats screamed that it should always take sixty votes to confirm a Supreme Court Justice, that this would change the rules forever and represent a danger to our democracy. But thirty seconds of research would tell a rookie reporter that two of the current Justices, Alito and Thomas, were both confirmed with less than sixty votes.

But that's one of those "inconvenient truths" which gets shoved under the rug. When you leave out a key fact like that, you're creating fake news.

Mainstream Media News Director: Okay, need a few more sidebars on the Supreme Court nomination and how the Republicans are about to do something dangerous with this nuclear option thing. The Democrats are burning up my phone.

Reporter: Sir, what about the Biden Rule?

News Director: Nobody cares what Joe said twenty-four years ago.

Reporter: But it makes the Democrats look like hypocrites.

News Director: Forget it. I deleted the video from the archives anyway. We need to show the Republicans are setting a dangerous precedent by possibly confirming a Supreme Court Justice with less than sixty votes.

Reporter: But Sir, two of the current Justices got less than sixty.

News Director: Old news, and no one is gonna remember that unless we tell 'em. And we're not gonna tell 'em.

And there are plenty of other "rules don't apply to us" examples, the prime example of which being politicians like the Kennedys being revered like saints while their serial womanizing is conveniently overlooked. Hell, Ted Kennedy, the so-called "Lion of the Senate" was actually a Presidential candidate despite the Chappaquiddick incident. Don't get me wrong, there have been plenty of Republicans who have been caught doing the same thing, and they're no saints either, but it seems like the liberals get a pass as long as they can win elections. (With the exception of Anthony Weiner, who created a story even the most talented fiction writer can't make up.) It's sorta like the bad boy quarterback who ends up in jail a few times but still has a job because he can help his team win.

It's up to reporters to present all the facts, especially since they love portraying politicians as "flip-floppers" and broadcasting video showing them doing an about-face. To be fair, Republicans flip-flop as much as Democrats. But their flips are always covered and thrown back in their faces, while the liberals often get a pass. You can't have it both ways, and very often the mainstream media conveniently forgets the file tape if the subject is someone they like.

You see, when it comes to members of the mainstream media and fake news, the rules don't apply to them either.

CHAPTER EIGHTEEN:

SOURCES SAY

If you've never seen the movie "All the President's Men" then you should spend a couple hours watching this gem. Terrific film, and one that inspired many young people to go into journalism. It's the tale of the reporters who broke the Watergate story back in the seventies with the help of the ultimate unnamed source, the guy known as Deep Throat. The movie depicts a lot of old fashioned legwork, tracking down leads, confirming information. It's old school reporting. And while the reporters are working the story, they have a really tough time getting people to go on the record. Nixon's Press Secretary calls them out for using rumors and unnamed sources. At one point, Jason Robards, who won an Academy Award playing their editor, wonders aloud when someone will actually go on the record.

That was then.

This is now.

And now, you don't need anyone to go on the record in order to have a lead story or one on the front page. Many times you don't even need any hard facts. Or any facts at all. But there are ways for you as a viewer or reader to get the heads-up that a possible bogus story is headed your way. How will you know? The reporter will tell you.

Here are some catch phrases currently being used for stuff that isn't on the record which might fall into the fake news category:

"A high level source tells me..."

"The word around Capitol Hill is..."

"Those in the White House close to the situation are said to have..."

"People with intimate knowledge of the meetings say..."

Notice the common denominator? Everything is simply rumor or hearsay, with no attribution. No quote in the newspaper, no sound bite on television. Never a name, not even a hint of who the "source" might be.

Because the source either didn't want to be revealed, which is fine.

Or doesn't even exist. Which isn't.

Hell, maybe that White House source is "close" to the situation because he works in the kitchen. Perhaps the "word" around Capitol Hill comes from a tourist.

And as one of my old news directors used to say, "You got no one on the record, you got no story."

While every reporter has sources, they're usually people who point you in the right direction or tip you off on something. Then it's up to you to confirm whatever lead you're given with hard facts and people who will go on the record. If you don't have either, you've got no story. So you wouldn't "quote" a source unless you could back it up with facts.

Well, that used to be the way things worked in the news business.

Now, I imagine a lead story can come from something like this:

Reporter (picking up phone and calling a congressional intern): Hey, Bob, how's it going over there?

Intern: Great, thanks so much for getting me this gig. Even though I spend most of my time getting coffee and running errands.

Reporter: Don't worry, once they learn you're smart they'll give you important stuff to do. So, if you remember our deal... you, uh, got anything for me?

Intern: Sorry, not much. I heard some raised voices when I was in the room next to the office of the Speaker of the House. I know that's not anything you can use.

Reporter: Actually...

And now the reporter has a "scoop" that the "Republicans are in turmoil with heated arguments involving the Speaker of the House." Of course those raised voices may have been a bunch of people yelling at a speakerphone that wasn't working correctly. Or members of Congress weren't even there and the loud chatter was between two contractors updating the telephone lines. And the "source" is an intern who's a college freshman with valuable experience running to Starbucks. Doesn't matter. There were raised voices in a key office and that sounds like there was an argument, so let's go with it. Which ends up as the lead story, front page news, and the main topic of a panel discussion on a Sunday morning show.

This will then be followed up with questions thrown at the Speaker about his party being in disarray, followed by mainstream media commentators wondering if we should believe his contention that everything is fine. After all, there *was* an argument in his office.

You don't tune into a news program or buy a newspaper for rumors. So if you see or read a story that seems to be filled with a lot of unnamed sources and rumors while not a single person has gone on the record, there's a chance the story falls into the fake news category. While sometimes sources give you the truth and some rumors turn out to be fact, unless the reporter has hard facts to back up the story, you should take it with a grain of salt until the facts emerge.

CHAPTER NINETEEN:

RUSSIAN TO JUDGMENT, OR, HOW TO BEAT A DEAD HORSE IN A NEWSROOM

"In a bombshell video from the Senate cafeteria, the Attorney General was seen putting Russian dressing on his salad. And we haven't been able to confirm this, but the clear liquid in his glass may have been vodka."

It's often called "death by sidebar" in a newsroom.

That's when you beat a story to death down to the molecular level. Even though it's already dead and there's absolutely nothing left to say.

You've seen it before, plenty of times, usually in cheesy tabloid shows or afternoon syndicated fare. Often it is something to do with the mysterious death of a Hollywood star, which offers a virtual sidebar buffet of possibilities. It goes through a news cycle, like those five stages of grief. Only these would be the first five stories.

-Breaking news: Anna Nicole died.
-How did Anna Nicole really die?
-Anna Nicole's dying deathbed confession!
-The shocking autopsy of Anna Nicole!
-Anna Nicole's funeral.
But wait! There's more!
-Anna Nicole is still dead!

Then, after we've gotten through the five sidebars of death and a broadcast executive realizes that Anna Nicole's story is worth big ratings even though she reached room temperature weeks ago, she's exhumed like a body dug up in a horror movie. And then the poor woman gets to die again, this time via satellite by sidebar.

It's the same deal with the Russians and the election. Since the Democrats cannot face the reality of why they lost the 2016 election, they needed something that goes beyond internal finger pointing. It couldn't possibly be the fault of the candidate, or the campaign staff, or the people who produced the TV ads. No way was it because the candidate was totally outworked by her opponent or that her primary opponent got the shaft and his supporters were angry. And you can't blame the voters because the candidate will need them again in the future. She can have her head frozen like Ted Williams and get thawed out in the year 2254 when the country will surely be in the mood for a liberal and the term "heads of state" will be taken literally.

There had to be a logical explanation why the Democrats lost.

They needed a bad guy.

And not just a name.

A villain that everyone will immediately accept. A sinister group, evil, with no moral compass. Led by a guy who rides horses without a shirt.

The Russians.

In the ultimate irony, the candidate who might have been sunk by her own emails found the perfect bad guys because of them.

Those leaked emails? Surely Wikileaks got them from the Russians, who desperately wanted a Republican President. No matter that it makes no sense since the Russians pretty much did what they wanted during the previous administration and probably could have continued to do the same. No matter that the Democrats never denied the content of the emails. No matter that (as of this writing) there's no physical proof. It's an old fashioned Cold War narrative that sounds juicy enough for the media to run with it and find every possible angle to keep it alive.

For as long as it takes.

Death by sidebar.

And this campaign could run longer than *War and Peace*. Problem is, many viewers are finding it's getting to be almost as boring as a Russian novel.

News Director: What's new with the Russia thing?

Reporter: The wife of a Republican Senator posted a recipe for Beef Stroganoff on her Facebook page.

News Director: Aha! Another connection. I'll bet she got that recipe from a Russian spy working to undermine the election! And we need to stake out all Russian restaurants in Washington to get video of Republicans who eat there.

Reporter: And, come to think of it, I did see one of those Russian nesting dolls in the office of a Congressman.

News Director: That's probably how the Russians are passing secret messages. We need to get that doll and open it up.

Reporter: And, you know that member of the cabinet who mentioned that she's a big Star Trek fan?

News Director: What about her?

Reporter: I have her on tape saying Chekov is her favorite character.

So how do you know what's fake news in this case?

First consider the amount of coverage given to the story. Hey, remember all the news stories you heard when the United States tried to influence the Israeli election in 2015 because some people wanted Benjamin Netanyahu out of office? You don't? Well, that's because it's okay for Democrats to fiddle with foreign elections. And while Russian influence may be a legit story, the sheer volume of coverage should tell you something. Because so far, none of the coverage has been based on hard evidence despite the endless ongoing investigations by various government agencies and Congressional committees. If nothing else, we discovered the country has seventeen intelligence agencies. (Still waiting for a reporter to explain why.)

But Russian interference provides a perfect narrative to make Republicans look bad. And look like they cheated. With the help of a really bad man who is easily portrayed as a comic book villain.

(By the way, if you've never heard about the Democrats asking a foreign country to get involved in an American election, go ahead and Google "Ted Kennedy Russia 1984" and see what you get. Interesting how no one ever brings that up. Then again, Teddy would be canonized like a saint if Congress ever decided to act like a Pope.)

The Russian angle has all the elements to create negative publicity for conservatives. It's easy to keep the story going, as it's brought up every week on the Sunday morning shows. And it's a convenient excuse for the 2016 result, because the Democrat couldn't possibly have lost a fair election.

At least that's what the mainstream media keeps telling us.

CHAPTER TWENTY:

ANTI-SOCIAL MEDIA

If you're familiar with the Terminator films, you know about Skynet, the computer system that becomes "self-aware" and basically tries to exterminate humanity to take over the planet.

So much for fiction: Skynet is actually here.

It's called social media.

And it didn't even need to employ time travel or Arnold Schwarzenegger.

Next to media bias, perhaps nothing has done more to divide the country than the absolute hate which permeates social media and the entire internet. The fact that you can post anonymously makes it even worse since there are no repercussions. Comments that would get you a punch in the mouth if made to someone's face are fair game, as this "digital road rage" has no rules. Nothing is off the table and the gloves are always off. Check out the Twitter or Facebook feeds of politicians and you'll find a parade of f-bombs and other lovely terms of endearment.

But it's not just the nasty comments you'll find. It's more like what you *won't* find. Yes, bias crept into social media sites, many of which are now determined to rid the internet of fake news. Well, a certain *type* of fake news. Because it's so damaging to society. The profanity and hate are apparently okay, as long as they are targeted in a certain direction.

Of course, since different people have different ideas of what constitutes fake news, you can guess what's happening. The people running these sites determine what's fake and what isn't. Guess which way many of them lean politically and socially?

Social Media CEO: I have decided we need to take action regarding the problem of fake news that's all over our site. It's damaging the political process and confusing people. It's gotta go.

Board Member: I'm not sure it's possible to delete everything. Unless you want me to call that guy who installs basement servers.

Social Media CEO: (laughing) Good one. Anyway, we don't have to get rid of everything. We're going to get rid of half of it. I want any so-called stories putting conservatives in a good light to be deleted, and those making liberals look bad deleted. And we need to cancel the accounts of the people who post this stuff as well. In fact, send them a computer virus for good measure.

Board Member: So, let me get this straight... we're going to leave some of the fake news on the site if it's favorable to our cause?

Social Media CEO: Yes, but we won't be calling it fake news.

Board Member: But... won't we look like hypocrites if we leave some of the bogus stuff on the site?

Social Media CEO: Just tell people who complain that we're looking into it. After a few days perception becomes reality anyway, so deleting it at that point won't make any difference. The damage we seek will be done.

But, one of those "bad" fake news stories about Democrats sneaked through. Like the board member said, you can't delete everything. Remember "pizzagate", the urban legend that made the rounds in 2016 claiming the Democrats were running a child trafficking ring out of a pizza parlor? Ridiculous, right? Then again, people have become so distrustful of politicians that nothing seemed impossible.

While there were many fake news stories in 2016 about both candidates, this one got a ton of coverage because it made the Democrats look bad and really brought the fake news topic into the forefront. Suddenly the mainstream media was beside itself over the massive amount of fake news out there about the pizza parlor and they were determined to let the public know it was bogus and probably the work of the Republicans. Fake news was damaging the Democratic candidate's reputation!

(Short pause for you to spit your coffee.)

Didn't matter that there were just as many, if not more, bizarre tales about Republicans floating around social media, many of which looked like they belonged on a supermarket tabloid cover next to the photo of the space alien baby. The mainstream gang seized on this pizza with all the negative toppings, even doing polls about whether voters thought Hillary was involved. The polls, of course, showed that some people actually believed this.

Bottom line, the story was that fake news was hurting her campaign.

And that's when the social media head honchos decided to get tough on the concept.

Of course, their idea of getting tough is like a parent with twins buying one a new car for a sixteenth birthday while the other gets a greeting card.

And if you're not going to be objective when seeking out fake news to delete, well, you're part of the problem.

As for those hard-to-believe stories you see every day, just do a little research to find out if they're fake. And don't forget to consider the source.

CHAPTER TWENTY-ONE:

HOORAY FOR HOLLYWEIRD

Actor: a person who makes millions of dollars by pretending to be someone else while reciting words written by someone else.

Imagine if a CEO of a Fortune 500 Company sat down at a board meeting and addressed the group like this: "I have decided to implement a new business model. I think it will be most profitable to offend an entire half of the country so that they boycott our product. And that half consists of people who vote Republican. So I'd like everyone to start insulting all conservatives as much as possible. Hold nothing back. Imply that they're stupid and racist. As of today, the gloves are off. Really go out of your way to tick people off because we don't want them as customers."

And while Hollywood in itself is not a major corporation, it has basically adopted this method of doing business.

Just take a look at the Oscars, the Emmys, and every other award show. Back in the day hosts like Johnny Carson and Billy Crystal told actual jokes that were funny. Now the "jokes" are simple cheap shots at Republicans. Back in the day the winners would be gracious and thank all those who had helped them reach the pinnacle of the profession. Now the winners use their time to make angry political and social statements. Actors will slam conservatives at every award show and then expect them to pay ten bucks to see their movies. Which is like a guy knocking on your door, calling you an idiot, then asking if you'd like to buy his lawn service.

But those outspoken actors are only the obvious part of Hollywood's agenda. The other half of their campaign is much more subtle, almost subliminal in some cases. And they help to spread some of the fake news created by their friends in the mainstream media.

Pay close attention to what's being offered on television and at the movie theater. The liberal agenda has slowly crept into many productions. Sometimes it's blatantly obvious, like the show "Madam Secretary" which is about a woman serving as Secretary of State. (Gee, I wonder where a network got *that* idea?) Perhaps Hollywood thought that by portraying a woman serving in this cabinet position it would lay the groundwork for the future. People would naturally associate the competent fictional Secretary of State with a real former Secretary of State who was running for President. While that didn't work, rumor has it that they have a show in development for 2020 about a President with an unusual hairstyle who will be depicted as evil.

The less obvious campaign entails sneaking social and political messages into a show. Cops are shown using racial profiling, conservatives are bad guys. The characters who you think will be the terrorists turn out to be the saints. Diversity is paramount. Hollywood will go out of the way to check off as many boxes as possible.

Hollywood Producer: I do like your script, but I think it would play a lot better if you added a few more characters.

Writer: Really? Seems like there are plenty of characters as it is. I'd be worried the audience might get confused. But you're the one producing it, so I'm open to suggestion.

Producer: Well, we need a gay character, a transgender character, a good Muslim, a bad Christian, a narrow-minded Republican and a Democrat who saves the day.

Writer: But this is a cartoon about chickens.

Producer: So?

Writer: I'm not sure how I would write that stuff into a children's story.

Producer: Well, if you're worried about too many characters you could change the ones you already have. Make your rooster gay. Get rid of that romantic scene with the hen. Now they're just friends. They can go shopping.

Writer: You can't be serious.

Producer: You want your script produced or not?

If you think that's ridiculous, pay very close attention to the stuff your kids are watching. All sorts of subtle messages are hidden in plain sight if you look hard enough.

But the campaign may have finally run its course. In recent years, the general public has become wise to Hollywood's antics. But actors, bless their narcissistic hearts, will keep beating the drum because they believe the general public actually cares what they think. And studios will keep churning out "message movies" only to see them fail at the box office.

So what does Hollywood have to do with fake news? Well, when you see actors covered constantly by the mainstream media and booked as guests on news shows, it further dilutes any credibility of journalism. Nothing says "news maker" like someone who makes a living speaking words written by someone else. But the mainstream media believes, as actors do, that the audience cares about the opinions of Hollywood stars, as if their fame and fortune make them smarter than anyone else.

Now *that's* a good bit of fake news.

CHAPTER TWENTY-TWO:

TAG! YOU'RE IT!

"Mister Mayor, when did you stop embezzling money?"

That's an old newsroom line about the ultimate no-win question to be asked of a politician. Even if the Mayor referenced above is pure as the driven snow, simply asking the question plants doubt in the minds of the voters. He may be as squeaky clean as Tim Tebow, but now he wears the badge of dishonor like an invisible scarlet letter. Just adding the word "stop" to the question implies that he used to steal.

The Mayor in question has been tagged.

Nope, not the Facebook kind of tag. Or the game those of us of a certain age played in grade school. Or that label you're not supposed to tear off a mattress under penalty of law. It's more like a bloodsucking tick that won't let go. Or that annoying neighbor who sells Amway and won't stop trying to sign you up. In this case, the accusation is enough to destroy a reputation. And in the era of social media, once this "story" gets passed around, half the people who read it will believe it. They don't stick around for the denial, they only hear the accusation. Which is on page one. (The denial, days later, ends up on page 29 next to the obituaries.)

Tagging is one of the most effective methods used by the mainstream media to harm a candidate they don't like. Because, and this is important, those who watch the mainstream media *want* stuff to believe. As long as said stuff is a negative portrayal of a conservative.

In a way, it's like the old fashioned "whisper campaign" that politicians of both parties have used for years against their enemies. Simply plant the rumor that a certain candidate has something unsavory in his character, let it spread, and all of a sudden the candidate has been tagged.

Members of the mainstream media do the same thing, only it's broadcast or printed. Throw it on social media and let it go viral. And since we're in the era of twenty-four hour cable news and print media that is constantly updating throughout the day, the media will beat the drum over and over until it becomes a natural part of the conversation. And whenever their target is mentioned, the tag will always accompany the discussion.

Here's a perfect example. Remember the Senate candidate who got tagged with the label of "witch" after she mentioned that as a teenager she had once "dabbled" in witchcraft? In that case, she basically tagged herself, but once the mainstream media smelled blood in the water, the thing took on a life of its own. You couldn't read or see a story about her without it creating a mental image of the candidate wearing a black pointed hat and stirring a pot filled with all sorts of evil potions. In reality, the media was stirring the pot. Of course it was rarely mentioned that it happened *in high school* when kids experiment with all sorts of stuff. Hell, half the kids in my class probably tried to contact dead people with a Ouija board on Halloween. It got so bad the poor woman even did a campaign commercial saying she wasn't a witch. Of course she lost, which was the main objective of keeping the tag alive. And the media didn't mind throwing a dig every once in a while that the Republicans had nominated a witch for the US Senate, even though she wasn't a witch, but that's beside the point. (Really too bad that she wasn't a member of a coven, since she could have put one hellacious curse on the networks.) That's a perfect example of how a tag can destroy someone or a campaign. Or both. This may have actually been the first *literal* witch hunt by the media.

Ah, the witch hunt, which is the tagging process taken to another level.

Let's play *find the witch*.

So once the target has been tagged, it's up to the mainstream media to dig up more stuff in an effort to make the tag look even worse. In the case of our Senate candidate, they'd be digging up old high school classmates trying to find out some shred of evidence to make their case even stronger. And of course, this would be the lead story that would go something like this:

Reporter: In an exclusive interview with one of the candidate's high school classmates, it has been revealed that her "dabbling" into witchcraft went a lot further.

Classmate: I didn't really know her, we weren't friends or anything. But she had a reputation—

Reporter: Oh, she was that kind of girl—

Classmate: Don't put words in my mouth. She had a reputation as the most honest girl in the school. At least she was given that honor in the yearbook. Anyway, I only spoke to her once at the school's Halloween dance when we arrived at the punch bowl at the same time. Real nice girl. Very sweet.

Reporter: How appropriate that it was Halloween, considering. I'm assuming her costume was that of a witch.

Classmate: No, she was dressed as Dorothy from the Wizard of Oz.

Reporter: Aha! A movie with a witch in it! Actually, two witches!

Of course, they rarely find the witch in any journalistic witch hunt. But it keeps the narrative alive until it is no longer needed.

Not that they care about the tag they've basically tattooed on their victims, who will probably have it follow them the rest of their lives. But like a piece of chewing gum, the media will chew you up and spit you out, using anyone to further their agenda.

Because it's okay to damage someone's reputation as long as it's in the name of fake news.

In the old schoolyard game of tag, if you were "it" you could simply get rid of the title by tagging someone else.

In the media's game of tag, you're pretty much "it" forever.

CHAPTER TWENTY-THREE:

GOTCHA!

"I'm ready for the 'gotcha' questions and they're already starting to come. And when they ask me who is the president of Ubeki-beki-beki-beki-stan-stan I'm going to say, you know, I don't know. Do you know? And then I'm going to say how's that going to create one job?"
    -Former Presidential candidate Herman Cain

The answer to Mr. Cain's question, "Do you know?" can be answered simply in regard to any gotcha question.

Chances are the reporter asking the question knows the answer.

Chances are also good the reporter didn't know the answer until he looked it up. Because the question wasn't even relevant or important. Now there's nothing wrong with a reporter doing research, which is something all news people should do every day. But if you're doing it for the explicit purpose of coming up with a gotcha question, you're no longer doing your job.

You're laying a trap.

Fake news alert!

Nothing makes a politician look stupid more than being unable to answer a question he supposedly should know. (And of course, the reporter asking the gotcha question will be sure to tell the viewers the politician *should* know.) You can often expect the "reaction shot" of the reporter who is absolutely flabbergasted that the politician can't come up with the answer. The jaw drops and the eyes widen in shock.

Yes, politicians are supposed to be well versed in all sorts of domestic and foreign affairs, but even the most thorough official can't know everything. That's why Presidents have a cabinet and advisers. Those running for office spend a lot of time preparing for debates, so they'll be ready for almost anything. (Unless, you know, they get the questions in advance.)

They key is "almost." And "anything" is usually something they haven't planned for.

They can do a ton of homework on the important issues, but they can't prepare for the gotcha question. And that's why the gotcha question is so valuable to the mainstream media.

Here's how it works:

-News organization decides it is incumbent upon them to make someone look stupid.

-Reporter finds something totally obscure that the politician can't possibly know.

-Reporter asks question.

-Politician doesn't know.

-Reporter feigns shock.

-News organization runs the segment every time the person is mentioned to reinforce his stupidity.

-Goal achieved.

Herman Cain summed it up perfectly, better than any politician on the receiving end ever had. If, as a reporter, you have to look it up because you don't know the answer to a question that is totally obscure, you really shouldn't be asking the question.

What Mr. Cain did so brilliantly (even though he lost the primary) was to suggest that politicians who are hit with a gotcha question simply turn it around and make the reporter look stupid. Damn, what a concept. Gotta love that Herman Cain.

Reporter: "How would you create a relationship with the President of Quatchibooie? You know who I'm talking about, right?"

Politician: "No, but I'm sure you can tell me. What's the native language of that country, by the way? And what's the capital?"

Personally, I'd love to see something like this. (I'd also love to see the wife of a cheating politician haul off and slap him instead of doing the Tammy Wynette "stand by your man" thing, but that's a topic for another day.)

Back to the whole premise of the gotcha question and how it basically creates fake news out of the blue. The fake news being that the politician is not well informed enough for a particular office. That the politician might not be very bright. Or, if the reporter can get the exchange to go viral, make the person look downright stupid, which is the brass ring of gotcha questions.

And that jewel is called "a gaffe."

Of course it is incumbent on the reporter and news organization to make sure the world knows the politician couldn't answer a question he should know.

Meanwhile, the collateral damage of this tactic is that it makes the average viewer feel stupid since he doesn't know the answer. I like to consider myself pretty well informed and I do read a lot, but I'll admit that on many occasions I've heard a gotcha question and had to look up the answer, so please, don't feel stupid if you don't know either.

But if we look back at Herman Cain's quote, we might have the answer to ending the gotcha questions once and for all by turning the tables.

No, not by having politicians turn the tables on reporters.

By having the general public ask gotcha questions of media people.

(Ah, I see your eyebrows just went up. Interested?)

Let's say you're at some political event covered by the media. You get there early and see reporters you recognize getting set up.

Walk up, smile and say hello. Make sure to compliment the reporter. (People do this all the time and most media people love the attention. We're all suckers for a compliment.) Only this time, have your cell phone video camera ready. Then ask the reporter a gotcha question. The sheer embarrassment might make that reporter stop asking such questions.

So there's your assignment. Let's see what you come up with.

Call it the fake news boomerang.

CHAPTER TWENTY-FOUR:

ROOTING FOR SUCCESS & WORSHIPING FAILURE

Okay, let's be honest. We've all rooted *against* someone. Maybe you wanted Tonya Harding to fall on her ass in the Olympics, or A-Rod to strike out in the World Series. Or perhaps you wished for a company that took a political or social stand to go belly up. And who didn't pray for Bernie Madoff to be found guilty?

While we love to see an underdog rise to the top of the mountain, if that person does one thing that hits us the wrong way, our sentiments can turn. There's something in our makeup that often wants to see that person take a tumble down the mountain, bouncing several times like that "agony of defeat" ski jumper on the old Wide World of Sports show. (It's on YouTube if you're too young to remember.) It must be some insatiable need to see Karma to rear its ugly head and dish out payback to someone who deserves it.

And when it comes to politics, we often root against someone. It's a pretty good assumption you're rooting for failure on some level if you voted for "the lesser of two evils" because you didn't like either candidate. (Any reporter doing an exit poll hears that comment more than anything else.) And sometimes you're rooting against something hoping for something better in the future. Does the phrase "I'd love a woman President... just not *that* woman" ring a bell?

Politicians have so much coverage these days that every tiny flaw, every little mistake, can be exposed down to the molecular level. Marco Rubio takes a drink of water during a speech and suddenly he's the subject of ridicule, as if no one has ever taken a drink. And with the mainstream media's current agenda, they'll jump on every little thing they can find.

And many of those "little things" fall into the fake news category.

A perfect example of a fake news "flaw" that falls into the "rooting for failure" department was the story that Vice President Mike Pence once stated he didn't want to eat dinner in public alone with a woman who wasn't his wife. And while we all know Pence is a deeply religious guy who's been married a long time and his motivation was probably not to create some infidelity scandal, he got hammered for this. If you listened to the media, all of a sudden he didn't respect women enough to dine with them. He probably wouldn't even speak to them during office hours either. Time for the media to cue up another "war on women" scandal.

Apparently he was much worse than the numerous politicians who have had extramarital affairs.

Fake news at its worst. Think about it... slamming a guy who's faithful to his wife. I mean, what a horrible person he must be. Yet the most famous political womanizer in recent history is revered by the media, as is the wife who put up with his indiscretions while most women would have left skid marks running away.

Put yourself in the Vice President's shoes. You happen to be a faithful old-fashioned spouse in the public eye. Cell phones are everywhere and he's a public figure. Everyone at the restaurant is going to take a picture. Suppose he's at a business meeting with some attractive younger woman from the White House staff in a classy, dimly lit restaurant and someone snaps a photo of them together. Maybe he's handing her a document, she reaches for it and the angle of the photo makes it look like they're holding hands. All of a sudden he's cattin' around. You can almost see the headlines from mainstream media newspapers. "Pence having romantic dinner with smoking hot young blonde while wife is at a PTA meeting!"

Hell, even if he wasn't an old fashioned religious guy, it's a good policy to avoid even the appearance of impropriety.

But this is a prime example of using fake news to root for failure.

And in the case of the new administration, the mainstream media is creating the appearance of failure at every turn. There might be some new legislation the President signed or a Republican Congress passed that will make life better for everyone, and yet that story will head straight to the back burner or the trash can, replaced by something trivial provided by an unnamed source. The media has created the appearance of turmoil in the White House since day one of the administration. People hate each other, staffers are leaking classified stuff because they can't stand working there, loud arguments are a daily occurrence, the President is furious with someone, the staff is furious with him. At some point I expect we'll hear that there was a food fight in the dining room resulting in strands of linguine hanging from a chandelier, someone shoe polished the toilet seats in the Lincoln bedroom, a prankster smeared Vaseline on the doorknobs to the Oval Office, and the Secret Service is on the roof dropping water balloons on foreign dignitaries.

The one common denominator for the stuff that has hit the airwaves and the newspapers: no source on the record.

Again.

But that doesn't matter if you're rooting for failure. The game plan is simple; put out negative reports every single day to create the appearance of an administration in utter turmoil. The White House is obviously dysfunction junction. Doesn't matter that you don't have a single source. If it's a rumor it's fair game, and qualifies as fake news.

Of course, when something bad actually happens, they'll take things to another level and go wall-to-wall with coverage.

Newspapers will print blaring headlines with huge type not seen since "Japanese Bomb Pearl Harbor." If your television had sensory capabilities, you could smell the mainstream media making the popcorn.

Meanwhile, pay attention to the body language and inflection of the media while they're rooting for failure. They'll have a gleam in the eye, the level of snark will go up a notch. The unspoken words are "I told you so." The spoken words are done so with glee, upbeat and excited.

Of course the opposite happens when they don't get their way, or, what's even more fun to watch, when they ask leading questions and don't get the answer they wanted.

Reporter: You must be outraged that undocumented immigrants in your own neighborhood were being deported right in front of your children. They must have been traumatized.

Citizen: No, actually it's good that the kids can see what happens if you break the law. Teaches them right from wrong. I'm glad that ICE is cleaning up the street.

Annddd... cue the long face.

By the way, this only happens on live TV. If this is a taped interview, it will never hit the air. Or, to use one of the more popular excuses, it will be "edited for time."

Uh, you've got a twenty-four hour network. You can sorta run anything you want for as long as it takes to run it.

But when a live interview does go off the rails for the mainstream media, the "double box" is a liberal reporter's worst enemy. That's the term for a split screen, showing the media person on one side with the interview subject on the other. And the viewer has hit the jackpot if you can see the reporter's face when the leading question doesn't result in an answer that validates the reporter's beliefs.

Yes, rooting for failure can be obvious if success makes a reporter look like someone's run over his dog.

So fake news isn't only about content... it's about the way reporters act on television or the style they write in a newspaper. It's as easy to distinguish as a smile from a frown.

And if the new administration does well, expect a lot of frowns.

As far as rooting for the new President to fail, well... it's not a reporter's job.

And it seems downright un-American to root against your own country.

CHAPTER TWENTY-FIVE:

THE JOURNALISM TREE IN THE FOREST

Thought you might like to know how the stories that end up on your evening newscast are chosen.

Local stations and network news departments all have what is simply known as a "morning meeting" during which reporters and other news staffers "pitch" stories to the powers that be, which, in the case of television newsrooms, is usually the News Director. Most organizations like reporters to pitch what are known as "enterprise stories"; in other words, stories the reporter has come up with on his own without clipping something out of a newspaper or following up on something seen on another station. As a reporter, you always strive to break something new. You're taught it's better to be right than first, so you want to make sure whatever you pitch is accurate. So basically the meeting goes around the room as each reporter pitches, and often fights for, his or her story. Sometimes you make your point and get the assignment, sometimes you're turned down. Sometimes it gets pushed back to a later date if there's a lot of news happening.

And once everyone has made a pitch and others have offered opinions, the News Director decides which stories will be covered on that particular day, and those that won't. Of course things can change during the day, as breaking news will often result in a story being killed or postponed. That decision usually rests with the News Director as well. Every reporter has been pulled off a story to cover something else that the boss has deemed to be more important.

Yep, bottom line, what you see on your local or network newscast is very often the final decision of one person.

Over the years I've seen great stories killed despite heated arguments in their favor and totally lame stories lead the newscast. And I've seen a News Director's personal opinions filter into a newscast and drive the narrative.

The one thing viewers need to keep in mind is that a newsroom is not a democracy. It's a dictatorship. The rank and file can yell and argue all they want, but one person makes the final decision.

And that's why, in a media that is so polarized, the stories you see on one network are often completely ignored on the competition. A small handful of people are controlling the networks.

Lately it has become a daily occurrence regarding top stories. You can almost bet money that the major breaking news on a certain conservative network will be totally ignored by the entire mainstream media.

Because it doesn't fit the narrative.

Like the proverbial tree falling in the forest, if no one covers the story, did it really happen?

This is called "bias by omission." Basically ignoring a story because you don't like it, or, in many cases these days, one that makes the party you support look bad. I imagine the morning meeting at a mainstream media network goes something like this:

News Director: Okay, our ratings are in the toilet, half the country hates us and thinks we broadcast fake news. Need a big story today. A real one this time. Cathy, waddaya got?

Reporter: You're not gonna like it, Sir.

News Director: Is it a big story?

Reporter: Huge. Story of the year.

News Director: Well, I'm not clairvoyant, what is it?

Reporter: (looks down and lowers her voice) A, uh, very prominent Democrat was caught breaking into the Oval Office, stealing classified documents from the President's desk and then posting them on social media. He actually got the launch codes, grabbed that nuclear football briefcase from a sleeping Secret Service Agent and nearly sent a missile at China which would have started World War Three. Fortunately the President's daughter caught him in the act and kicked his ass.

News Director: Anyone break the story yet?

Reporter: Your favorite conservative network, Sir. They had a live shot from the hospital where they are surgically removing a stiletto heel from his butt. They've got team coverage and are going wall-to-wall.

News Director: Then we're not doing it. I don't even want to see it on the website. What else have you got?

Reporter: Uh, all I've found is a veteran Republican Congressman who accepted a free meatball sandwich during a campaign rally in Little Italy back in 1994 and didn't report it on his campaign disclosure form.

News Director: I dunno... wait, did you say this happened in Little Italy?

Reporter: Yeah.

News Director: Aha! We can tie him to the Mafia. Say he's getting kickbacks from the Mob. Now that's a lead story!

Now, as to the degree of the bias by omission, here's a good indicator. If a conservative news outlet breaks a story and the mainstream media touches on it but doesn't ignore it, that means the story isn't all that bad for liberals. If the mainstream media totally ignores a major story and it's obvious they're trying to change the subject, that means the story has merit and could be seriously damaging to the Democrats.

So does bias by omission constitute fake news? You betcha. You're not doing your job as a journalist if you fail to cover legitimate stories.

CHAPTER TWENTY-SIX:

IT'S TOO DAMN COLD FOR GLOBAL WARMING

"The National Weather Service now says this is the coldest winter on record. In a related story, Democrats are sponsoring a bill to officially change the term global warming to climate change, while reserving the right to change it back should we have a hot summer."

I wish I could be as dedicated to my beliefs as actor Leonardo DiCaprio is to his own. The guy is tireless fighting climate change, flying his private jet around the world to promote the cause. Burning several thousand pounds of jet fuel is an excellent way to show you really care about the environment. I mean, really, why fly commercial and have to share the same airplane with the great unwashed masses of coach class? The horror!

And it would be great to be so caring about the environment like the Dakota pipeline protesters who left a one-point-one million dollar trash cleanup bill for the taxpayers. Transporting oil across the land? Bad for Mother Nature. Tossing enough fast food wrappers, coffee cups and garbage to fill up 835 dumpsters on the supposedly pristine ground? No problem. Their message is the important thing.

Those two stories are examples of "hypocrite coverage" by which the negative part of the story simply doesn't make the cut. You can find plenty of sound bites from DiCaprio harping on the environment, and lots of video of the pipeline protesters suffering in the bitter cold while they try to save the unspoiled land, but you rarely see the seedy underbelly of these stories. Because that would not be protecting the narrative. After all, conservatives are the ones who don't care about the environment. The liberals will tell you so, as they tool around in limos and chauffeur their kids all day rather than buy them each a bicycle.

In this case, the mainstream media isn't covering the negative aspects of these stories, pretending they don't exist.

Like they're fake.

See, fake news isn't only about stories that aren't true. It's also about telling one side. And if you only tell one side of a story (here's that pesky first class of Journalism 101 rearing its ugly head again) then... wait for it...

You. Don't. Have. A. Story.

Remember when some members of the previous administration suggested that people who denied climate change could be prosecuted? Reminded me of that original *Star Trek* pilot where the aliens punished people for "wrong thinking." Normally this would be a huge story. Seriously, our government taking legal action against free speech? Having an opinion is now breaking the law? And most reporters don't go wild over this story? If a Republican administration had done this the mainstream media's collective heads would explode, comparing it to Nazi Germany. But this side of the story was pretty much ignored, because... wait for it... it didn't fit the narrative. Imagine if that directive had actually become law.

Conservative reporter walking past federal agent: Morning, Agent Jones. Beautiful day, huh?

Agent: It's hot as hell.

Reporter (laughing): You must have the flu. It's 72 degrees.

Agent: Are you denying the planet is burning up?

Reporter: I just said it was a beautiful day—

Agent: Up against the wall, hands behind your back. You have the right to remain silent.

Reporter: What's the charge?
Agent: Climate change denial. Enjoy your life in the slammer.
Blasphemer!

Of course at this point the previous administration would have contacted Hollywood to sell the rights to a new superhero movie titled "Agent Jones, Thought Police" with all the profits going to fight climate change. The talking action figure would tell children, "go build a windmill." (Meanwhile, the game of Monopoly would be banned since it implies that people with the most money are winners.)

Now if it's a slow news day in the climate change world, the media has a literal "true north" in the form of the Arctic. Nothing says the planet is getting warmer better than that file footage showing part of a glacier sliding into the ocean. Yep, when that ice melts all the Atlantic and Pacific Ocean beaches will be gone and people in Kansas will all soon own waterfront property.

Now you're probably saying, hey, that video doesn't lie and it does look like the ice at the North Pole is indeed melting. But you probably haven't seen the other side of the story thanks to the fake news premise that anything not contributing to the climate change narrative should not be covered.

That other side of the story which is rarely mentioned? The ice at the South Pole. Yep, the Antarctic sea ice is growing. That's not some conservative talking point, but from a study done by NASA. So is the ice lost at the Arctic balanced out by the ice gained at the other end of the planet? Does it mean those people in Kansas can put that deep sea fishing boat purchase on the back burner?

Remember, it's not news if you aren't telling the whole story. The climate change thing can be debated forever, with facts backing up both sides. But you can't cherry pick your facts to promote your agenda. A real news story gives you all the angles.

Since the mainstream media is only telling you one side, it qualifies as fake news.

CHAPTER TWENTY-SEVEN:

IT'S PLANTING SEASON

"When I give you this signal, I'm gonna throw some stuff on the fan."

-local politician to a TV news photographer

I was a young reporter at a new job, out on a story with a veteran photographer who had been around the block many times. Since I wanted to learn as much as possible from the experienced people in the newsroom, I kept quiet and followed his lead. We'd already wrapped up our story and the station asked us to swing by a school board meeting to pick up a quick sound bite. The reporter covering education was tied up on something else.

As we were setting up before the meeting, one of the board members came up to the photographer and gave him the heads up that all hell was gonna break loose when she scratched her nose. Fast forward through a mind-numbing meeting which has not inspired any of the photogs to record anything. Suddenly she looked right at him and gave the signal. He framed up the camera on her and hit the record button. As soon as the little red light atop the camera went on she launched into a tirade with a great sound bite.

And of course, we were the only ones to record it in its entirety.

Yep, we'd been used.

Welcome to planting season. No gardening experience required.

Sure, we still would have gotten the story, but without the alert from the school board member the photog would have missed the first few seconds of the great sound bite.

Of course, that's not a true planted question by traditional definition. But it's awfully close.

When it's planting season, those are pretty obvious. For those of you with a green thumb, journalistic planting season runs year round. Lack of experience is definitely a plus from a politician's point of view. Think of politicians as the nursery doing the planting and the reporters providing the, uh, fertilizer.

It's a simple plan, really, and works pretty often. A politician picks out a reporter who is both friendly to his cause and to him, then develops a relationship. When he needs something he gets in touch with the reporter, and asks the reporter to pose a specific question, no doubt about a topic on which the politician is passionate and will have a great response written in advance and memorized word for word. Fast forward to a news conference. The politician calls on the friendly reporter, who asks the planted question about what is surely a hot button issue, often something no other reporter has heard about, and presto, the politician has a great answer. Now the other reporters have realized their big story of the day has changed and are scrambling to come up with follow-up questions.

Suddenly, something totally off the radar is the lead story on every newscast.

A good example was that "beer summit" issue several years ago. A White House reporter brought up an incident hardly anyone had heard about, and of course the response was perfect and stirred the pot. Which was the whole point since it was a hot button issue. Result, lead story for several days. While there's no proof the question was planted, it looked funny. And most viewers could figure it out as well. I watch a lot of news and I hadn't heard about it.

There are other plants that may or may not get results, often perpetrated on rookie or lazy reporters who don't bother to check things out. Those are the ones politicians like to test. Often they'll target the new person in town, figuring the reporter wants to make a great first impression breaking a big story.

Here's how it works from a reporter's point of view. You'll get an anonymous call with incredible dirt on some politician, and the caller expects you ask a specific question and run the story. If you're a decent journalist you know right away that this is a plant and obviously came from the politician's opposition, so you check things out, and very often discover there's nothing to the story. Or at least another side. If you're inexperienced or lazy (or both), you run with it without checking. And then have to face the music when you often find out it wasn't true because you didn't get the other side of the story and forgot the basic concept of journalism. The ultimate result is that fake news has hit the air.

But, as we say in TV news, by that time the story has "gone to Pluto." On the airwaves in outer space, leaving the solar system at warp speed. You can't unscramble an egg. Retractions? Who pays attention to those? Especially when they're a throwaway line at the end of the newscast. "By the way, that lead story we had yesterday? Never mind."

By that time the general public has seen it and is already talking about it since you can't put the genie back in the bottle. True or not (most often not) it has made an impression and reached its goal.

So how can you recognize the planted question?

Look for a few things.

First, the question is obscure and seemingly out of the blue, something that has never been brought up before. If you look it up on the internet you can't find much of anything.

Second, the politician has a perfect answer ready, even though no one else has ever heard of the topic.

Third, no other reporter at the news conference follows up. Because they haven't heard of it either. It's a bonus if you get a shot of the press corps looking puzzled.

While it may or may not be fake news, it's a way for politicians to manipulate the media and create a headline where none should exist. And very often the members of the media are all too happy to get an exclusive that has been dropped in their lap. A win-win for the politician and the mainstream media, while the general public loses because they are, in effect, being used. Just as I was as a rookie reporter.

In this case, the reporter gets credit for "breaking the story" even though it was handed to him and required no reporting skills at all.

And that's not just fake news, it is fake reporting.

CHAPTER TWENTY-EIGHT:

FAKE NEWS TEST

(Actually, this is a real test about fake news)

Okay, boys and girls, time to see what you have learned so that you may go out into the world and share with the rest of the class.

Answers are multiple choice, which will no doubt offend supporters of Common Core.

1. How do you know if a mainstream media reporter is *definitely* broadcasting fake news?

A. The story sounds fishy

B. The reporter is known to be biased

C. The network has an obvious agenda

D. His lips are moving

2. How many mainstream media reporters does it take to change a 100 watt incandescent light bulb?

A. One. It's a simple task.

B. Two. One consumer reporter to do a story on incandescent light bulbs effect on climate change, then one to call Al Gore to ask for advice.

C. Three. One to find the date the light bulb was installed, one to find a connection to a previous Republican administration, one to do a story blaming Republicans.

D. Several. One to find a therapist for the reporter who notices the bulb is of the dreaded incandescent variety, one to check the current government regulations on light bulbs in places of business, one to alert a union electrical crew of four needed to replace the bulb, one to carry the bulb to a White House dumpster, and one to do a story revealing the White House is breaking the law using 100 watt incandescent bulbs which will fry the planet.

3. Which story is the mainstream media least likely to cover?

A. Hard evidence showing climate change is bogus.

B. A liberal caught stealing campaign funds.

C. Confirmation that Republican members of Congress give more to charity than Democrats.

D. A Republican President finds a cure for cancer.

4. What is a mainstream media reporter's favorite safe space?

A. An Ivy League college.

B. A California university.

C. Covering the Democratic National Convention.

D. The newsroom.

5. What is the worst micro-aggression a mainstream media TV reporter can endure?

A. Having a Press Secretary refer to a group of male and female reporters as "you guys."

B. Being roped off by a candidate while trying to cover a campaign.

C. Working with someone who didn't attend an Ivy League college.

D. Being called "fake news."

6. How does a mainstream media meteorologist describe a sunny, 72 degree day in a weather forecast?

A. A perfect day.

B. Chamber of Commerce weather.

C. Great afternoon to be outdoors.

D. Blistering heat.

7. If a story breaks in which a gay baker refuses to make a wedding cake for a Muslim couple, which side will the mainstream media support?

A. The baker

B. The couple.

C. They'll simply report the story and not take sides.

D. The entire news department will go into vapor lock and be unable to make a decision.

8. When doing an exit poll in Chicago, where is a mainstream media reporter most likely to gather favorable results for Democrats?

A. Outside a polling place in a liberal district.

B. At the local courthouse.

C. At City Hall.

D. At a cemetery.

9. What is the mainstream media's definition of "voter fraud?"

A. Someone who votes twice.

B. Someone who votes and is not a US citizen.

C. Someone who votes using the name of a dead person.

D. A Republican winning a Presidential election.

10. What's the definition of a diverse staff at a mainstream media network?

A. Half of the employees are women, half are men.

B. All minorities are represented on the staff.

C. A good mix of veterans and rookies.

D. Hiring a conservative to run the mail room.

The correct answer for each question is "D" and a passing grade for conservatives is 100.

CHAPTER TWENTY-NINE:

STEREOTYPES: THE VERY WORST PART OF FAKE NEWS

Perhaps the biggest effect of a biased media and fake news is that it has resulted in a divided country. I'm not sure if America has ever been this polarized in our lifetime, and you can trace it directly to the stereotypes perpetrated on us by those in the news business.

Of course, those in the news business would argue that stereotypes are never accurate. Yet they keep labeling people as if we're all the same according to the way we vote.

I have very liberal friends, very conservative friends and moderate friends who are very independent. The one common denominator they all have is that they're good people. Otherwise they wouldn't be my friends. Personally, I don't give a damn how they voted or what their opinions are on religious or social issues.

I've known gay Republicans and black conservatives, pro-life Democrats and liberals who loved guns. Members of any political party are not all in total lock-step with everything on that party's platform. You can be a Democrat and be against gay marriage. You can be a Republican and drive an electric car because you are passionate about the environment.

Having covered many politicians as a reporter, I can tell you there are good Democrats and bad Democrats, good Republicans and bad Republicans. And to illustrate how wrong reporters can sometimes be about politicians, two guys who I thought were really sincere (one from each party) are now in jail. You really never know what's in someone's heart, which is why we judge people by their actions.

I've written several political novels. Some have good liberal main characters and some have good conservative main characters. Because that's the way real life is. You don't paint everyone with the same broad brush.

But the media would have you believe that all conservatives spend their time burning crosses on their lawns, painting swastikas on churches and dumping radioactive waste in our waterways. They'd have you believe that all liberals hug trees all day while harboring Syrian refugees in their basements and heating their homes by burning American flags. The mainstream media loves to pick out a small segment of the population and portray these people as representative of an entire party or age group or religion. The overwhelming majority of Americans, liberal and conservative, are normal people trying to make life better for themselves and their families. Most are actually too busy to pay much attention to what's going on in Washington. But the biased coverage they do see has been going on for so long it's gotten ingrained in our beliefs that all Democrats are the same and so are all Republicans. And the media wants you to look down on someone who doesn't think like you do, even as their members profess tolerance. The most intolerant people in the country seem to be some members of the media.

Pretty hypocritical, huh?

People vote the way they do for many different reasons. Many vote their pocketbook. A lot of people vote for the lesser of two evils, basically casting a ballot against someone. But bottom line, people generally support someone who they think will make things better. Bear in mind that the definition of what is actually "better" differs with every person. Maybe a good job is most important to you. Maybe it's the environment. Perhaps it's immigration. Or some other issue you're passionate about. And a lot of people vote for a candidate who is simply more likable.

Doesn't really matter. You vote for what you consider to be important. That doesn't make you smart or stupid, good or bad. That shouldn't make you hate your neighbor because that person voted for a different candidate than you did or has a yard sign supporting someone you don't like.

But fake news is as destructive as anything when it comes to things which drive us apart. If America is to come together, as politicians like to say, people must ignore the media-created stereotypes and stop labeling their neighbors according to their political views. Or their age. Or religion. Or opinions on various issues.

Politicians of both parties fail to grasp one basic concept as they often try to ram their beliefs down our throats:

You can't legislate thought.

The media needs to realize the same thing.

CHAPTER THIRTY:

THE FUTURE OF FAKE NEWS

Hopefully, you realize this book is simply a very sarcastic and satirical shot at the mainstream media people who simply do not act as responsible journalists.

That's not to say all media people have gone off the rails.

I know plenty of reporters, anchors and executives, liberal and conservative, who believe in the basic rules of objectivity. Unfortunately, most of them are not in the decision-making positions at the networks or major newspapers.

And most of them, like myself, believe it is not our job to tell you what to believe and what not to believe. Our job is not to change opinions, or push political agendas. Who are we to tell you how to think? What gives a reporter that right? Or anyone, for that matter?

Our job is to put the facts as we know them in front of you. And to get as many of those facts as we can from as many sides as possible. Very often there are more than two sides to an issue. Stories are not always black and white, but have many shades of gray. You as the consumer of news can then consider the facts and make your own decisions.

What can you do to stop fake news? Well, there are ways to send a message. Television networks and local stations need ratings to be profitable, and if you stop watching, they'll lose advertising dollars. You can avoid products being advertised on fake news outlets. Newspapers and magazines are already on life support and you can read most of them online for free anyway. But do you still have a subscription to a publication printing what you consider to be fake news? Cancel it. Or one that is supposed to cover sports but can't resist throwing a dig at politicians? Outta here. I recently canceled a 30 year subscription to Sports Illustrated because of that. And do you follow a blog which seems to be filled with stories that don't seem quite right? Stop following.

Nothing sends a message better than hitting someone in the wallet.

And nothing hits a reporter in the soul more than being considered one without any credibility.

Meanwhile, support those news organizations that are objective, that cover both sides of the story, that present facts rather than opinions. Hopefully in the near future powerful positions in the mainstream media will be filled by people who actually follow the rules of journalism.

Till then, do your best to separate the truth from fiction.

And if you're curious as to where my personal opinions lie on political, religious or social issues... well...

I won't tell you. And I won't tell you how to think either.

That's not my job.

About the Author

Nick Harlow has spent 30 years in the television news business as a reporter, anchor and manager for local stations and as a freelance field producer for all the major networks. He is one of the few people in the country who does work for both NBC and Fox News. He also took a few years off to work on political campaigns. He also runs a mentoring business for young journalists.

Nick is the author of seven political thrillers and a few journalism books.

Made in the USA
Lexington, KY
01 June 2017